Beautifully written, Pam's reflections on the stories behind our much loved hymns are truly inspiring, reminding us of God's faithfulness, presence and grace in our daily lives.

Dave Bilbrough, songwriter and contemporary worship leader

Pam Rhodes seems to me the ideal author for such a refreshing book as this. Over the past decades, presenting Songs of Praise *for the BBC, her empathy and skill have brought us moving stories of spiritual and human experience, often related to the words of a hymn. By drawing on these interviews, together with her own reflections on (mostly) familiar hymns, she brings to the page a warmth and freshness which enable these hymns to lift our hearts to God and point us again to Jesus.*

From her long experience as a presenter on Songs of Praise, *Pam Rhodes explores the place of hymns in the spiritual and human stories of some of those interviewed. This unique background, and the freshness of the writing, combine to offer us a different and very welcome kind of book about familiar hymns.*

Love so Amazing *displays the warmth, freshness and evident love of hymns that we have come to expect from such a favourite presenter of* Songs of Praise.

Bishop Timothy Dudley-Smith, hymnwriter

Pam Rhodes brings a warm personal touch to the telling of some great stories about the greatest hymns.

Sally Magnusson, journalist, broadcaster and writer

Love
So Amazing

40 reflections on my favourite hymns

Pam Rhodes

MONARCH
BOOKS

Oxford, UK & Grand Rapids, Michigan, USA

Published by Monarch Books
an imprint of
Lion Hudson plc
Wilkinson House, Jordan Hill Road,
Oxford OX2 8DR, England
Email: monarch@lionhudson.com
www.lionhudson.com/monarch

ISBN 978 0 85721 570 3
e-ISBN 978 0 85721 571 0

First edition 2014

Acknowledgments
Unless otherwise indicated, Scripture quotations taken from the Holy Bible, New International Version Anglicised. Copyright © 1979, 1984, 2011 Biblica, formerly International Bible Society. Used by permission of Hodder & Stoughton Ltd, an Hachette UK company. All rights reserved. "NIV" is a registered trademark of Biblica. UK trademark number 1448790. Scripture quotations marked KJV from The Authorized (King James) Version. Rights in the Authorized Version are vested in the Crown. Reproduced by permission of the Crown's patentee, Cambridge University Press. Scripture quotations marked ESV are from The Holy Bible, English Standard Version® (ESV®) copyright © 2001 by Crossway, a publishing ministry of Good News Publishers. All rights reserved.

Further acknowledgments on p. 160.

A catalogue record for this book is available from the British Library

Printed and bound in the UK by Clays Ltd, St Ives plc, September 2014, LH26

Contents

Introduction

ou could have knocked me down with a feather when the publishers asked me to compile this book of devotional thoughts which could be used as an aid to prayer throughout the year. I was delighted because I've often enjoyed using collections like this myself. I was just surprised they asked me. Surely they would be better to choose someone trained in theology and ministry – someone who is likely to know the answers – rather than me, who has spent many years as a presenter on BBC Television's *Songs of Praise*, asking the questions?

But the questions I ask are answered by people who are generous and brave enough to share their private, sometimes painful experiences with *Songs of Praise* viewers, in the hope that the lessons they've learned along the way might be of help to others. Inevitably, they are. The people I interview on the programme are seldom professional speakers. They are mostly ordinary folk, your neighbours and mine, who are extraordinary in the way that each and every one of us is. Each of us has a story to tell, our own challenges to face – and yet, because we all share the experience of being human, our feelings are often much the same, whatever our individual circumstances.

We can learn a lot from others who have had to cope with difficult times of bereavement, illness, disappointment, fear, or loneliness. When they speak of their sense of helplessness or doubt, we know just what they mean. When they go on to share their sense of God in the darkest times, we can be encouraged and reassured by their certainty that, even though it sometimes felt as if their prayers were going nowhere, God was there all the time, in the hurt and despair with them, guiding, protecting, and comforting them along the way.

So I have decided to draw on the experience and wisdom of others who, armed with faith, have faced whatever life has brought them, then shared their experience in the most evocative, touching, and memorable way – through writing hymns. Time marches on, and everyday life changes at an alarming rate – but I don't think the human experience changes much at all. Whether it's a psalmist waking up one morning 3,000 years ago feeling weary of the world and in need of guidance and comfort, or Stuart Townend or Graham Kendrick waking up today feeling world-weary and in need of comfort and guidance, are their emotions and reactions really so very different? As wordsmiths, they express those feelings in the most beautiful texts which, when matched with the right piece of music, become unforgettable treasures for the rest of us. That means that when we wake up feeling weary, without direction or comfort, we can find inspiration in the timeless thoughts of hymn writers. Hymns are prayers in our pockets, a spiritual first-aid kit that has its home among our memories. Just think of a hymn like "Abide with Me", written by Henry Lyte at a time when he knew his own death was imminent:

Abide with me, fast falls the eventide,
The darkness deepens, Lord, with me abide.

Can you think of a more beautifully worded prayer than that? And after years of singing that hymn, those words are so deeply embedded in our minds and hearts that Henry Lyte's prayer can be ours too, whenever we feel darkness is deepening around us. Hymns speak to us and for us, heart to heart, soul to soul, connecting us in fellow feeling to the writer, whoever they are and whenever they wrote.

Five centuries ago, the great Christian reformist Martin Luther already understood the power of the hymn book. He held up a Bible and declared, "This is the gospel." Then he raised his other hand, in which he held a hymn book, and said, "And this is how we remember it."

So this is a storybook of the very human experiences and feelings of the writers of some of our favourite hymns. What was going on in their lives as they wrote those lines which are stored with love in our memories? What sort of challenges were they facing that echo what we can relate to ourselves? And what might we learn from their lives which might help us with our own?

And why is the title of this book *Love So Amazing*? Because the common theme expressed in these hymns in answer to all the difficulties and challenges we face is God's love, expressed so eloquently by hymn writer Isaac Watts at the start of the eighteenth century in his hymn "When I Survey the Wondrous Cross". It is still every bit as true for each and every one of us today. He said God's amazing love "demands my soul, my life, my all".

Wow! What a challenge that throws out to us – but then, the words of hymn writers aren't always cosy and comfortable. They nudge our conscience and scrape away at our complacency. They remind us of the true demands of the Christian life. They spur us on to react and respond. Most of all, they remind us of the Almighty God who created the heavens and earth in all their vastness and complexity, but who also created us to be unique and precious through his divine and *amazing love*.

God Be with You Till We Meet Again

God be with you till we meet again;
By his counsels guide, uphold you,
With his sheep securely fold you:
God be with you till we meet again.

Till we meet, till we meet,
Till we meet at Jesus' feet;
Till we meet, till we meet,
God be with you till we meet again.

(Jeremiah E. Rankin: 1828–1904)

*I*n 1882, when Jeremiah Rankin, the minister of a congregational church in Washington DC, thought he could do with a hymn for his choir to sing as the congregation departed each week, he found himself thinking of the true meaning of the word *goodbye*. Looking in the dictionary, he discovered that it was short for *God be with you*. With that snippet of knowledge, he created a hymn which would become dear to those in fear, conflict, or deep sorrow for generations to come.

In fact, very soon after, this hymn took on life and death significance for soldiers fighting in the Boer War between the British Empire forces and the Dutch settlers in South Africa. Back at home, most of these men would have had a family copy of the Sankey hymn book which was known around the world and from which number 494, "God Be with You Till We Meet Again", was a text they kept in their hearts as they marched off to war. There is a very moving account written by one young British soldier about how the lads would meet in the "glory room" on any evening before they were due to go into battle. These tough men would shake each other's hands and whisper, "God bless you – 494", knowing that the significance of that number would be instantly recognized. He wrote:

> *These are Christian men parting from Christian men, and no one knows whether it will be in earth or heaven that he will meet his comrade next. And so night by night before each regiment takes its departure someone starts 494. Often with hands clasped and not without tears they sing:*
>
> *God be with you till we meet again,*
> *Keep love's banner floating o'er you,*

Smite death's threatening wave before you,
God be with you till we meet again.

They will not forget it, these soldier lads, and as
they pass one another on their long marches, or
as with rapid tread they advance to charge some
almost impregnable defence, they will shout to
one another, these Christian soldiers, 494 – God
be with you till we meet again!

Saying goodbye is never easy, especially when we're worried about where those we love are going or how long they will be gone. Somehow, knowing that the word *goodbye* is really a prayer for God's blessing makes the separation from those we love and miss more bearable.

This song was played as the curtain closed on my mother's coffin, and I still feel choked with sadness and loss when I think of that moment of farewell from the very best friend I've ever had. But with the blessing of these words, I knew that God was with her in death just as he had been her constant companion in life. And somehow the blessing was not just for her, but also for all of us who mourned her passing and wondered how we would manage in a world that didn't have her warmth and loving presence in it. God was with us. He would never leave us. There was infinite comfort and reassurance in that knowledge, a comfort that has remained with me ever since.

Father, stay with us always – in our fear, our uncertainty, our pain, and our sadness. Comfort us in the shelter of your love, and help us to show that same love in your name to others who need to feel the strength of your compassion and the certainty of your presence.

494

AMEN

Just as I Am

Just as I am, without one plea
But that Thy blood was shed for me,
And that Thou bidd'st me come to Thee,
O Lamb of God, I come.

Just as I am, though tossed about
With many a conflict, many a doubt,
Fightings and fears within, without,
O Lamb of God, I come.

(Charlotte Elliott: 1789–1871)

*U*ntil she reached her thirties, Charlotte Elliott led a happy, carefree life filled with much pleasure. She especially enjoyed portrait painting and was so skilled at it that her work became quite popular. And then, when she was thirty-two, she was struck down by an illness that was to rob her of her health and energy for every day of her life until she died at the age of eighty-two. It seems her illness caused a form of paralysis which meant that she could barely drag herself around her room. Her limbs ached so much that lying in bed was all she could manage. It's hardly surprising that she struggled with deep depression, frustration, and hopelessness.

There were times when she felt particularly useless, like the day in 1834 when her brother, a vicar in Brighton, was organizing a bazaar to raise funds for a much-needed school to educate the children of poor clergymen. The whole household was swept up in the preparations and was too busy to notice Charlotte's increasing despair at not being able to join in and contribute in some meaningful way. She felt abandoned not just by the family, but also by God – and these thoughts were so shocking that she comforted herself by thinking of the reasons she knew in Scripture that would help her remember that God's love was constant and faithful. She thought about how Christ's blood was shed for her and how God has promised to receive all who come to him in faith – and, being a poet, she started to write the first lines of this hymn. In the verses that follow, she poured out her own sense of inadequacy in the knowledge that, despite her limitations, she was as precious and loved by God as anyone else.

She managed to get the poem published, and was glad because she thought she could contribute any proceeds to her brother's school fund. The poem was instantly successful and was soon selling across Britain in large numbers as well as being translated into a number of foreign languages.

Years later, her brother said that, through her words, not only had Charlotte raised a great sum of money, but she had also managed to touch the hearts of more people when they were feeling helpless and alone than he could ever achieve in his whole career as a minister!

During her lifetime, Charlotte wrote several hundred hymns which appeared in books with titles such as *The Invalid's Hymn Book* and *Hours of Sorrow Cheered and Comforted*. Her verses empathize with those who suffer from grinding depression and ill health because she speaks from experience. Even now, nearly two centuries after "Just as I Am" was written, it resonates down the years, connecting with fellow sufferers who live with constant pain and disability. Charlotte recognizes their doubts and inner conflict. She understands their sense of isolation and futility – and then she reassures them with her own certainty that God looks beyond the frail, tired body to love the very soul of them.

My body is weak, Lord. Sometimes the pain gets me down until it's almost too much to bear. There is such loneliness in illness. So I pray for your comfort and presence when I am at my lowest. Help me to see beyond the way I am now to recognize the person I really am. Give me the strength and determination to be all I can be.

Amen

What a Friend We Have in Jesus

What a friend we have in Jesus,
All our sins and griefs to bear!
What a privilege to carry
Everything to God in prayer!
O what peace we often forfeit,
O what needless pain we bear,
All because we do not carry
Everything to God in prayer.

(Joseph Scriven: 1819–86)

Joseph Scriven would probably be astonished to know that his words ever saw the light of day as a hymn, let alone that they bring comfort and encouragement to just about every Christian around the world! This obscure, devout man drew on his own experience of great sadness as he wrote these verses that echo in the life of everyone who hears them.

Joseph was born in the rolling hills of County Down in Northern Ireland, where he graduated from Trinity College in Dublin with the prospect of a wonderful life ahead. He was in love and due to marry the following day when the shocking news came that his beloved fiancée had drowned in an accident. Heartbroken, he decided that completely new surroundings might help his grief, so he set sail for Canada to take up a teaching post. You can imagine his delight when he fell in love again with Eliza, a relative of one his students. The couple soon set a wedding date – one that was never fulfilled because Eliza was suddenly struck down by a serious illness which claimed her life before their marriage could take place.

Having twice been robbed of the prospect of happiness, Joseph sank into depression and ill health, during which his only solace was prayer. He shared all his disappointment and worries with the Lord until he began to think of Christ as his best and most trusted friend. He balanced that with the need to work. By this time, he had settled in Port Hope, Ontario, where he managed a small dairy. Before long, he became known as the local "Good Samaritan" because he gave all his time, money, and even the clothes off his own back to help the poor and needy, spreading the love and compassion of Christ wherever he went.

But we would never have heard of this modest, humble man if it weren't for the short poem he wrote to comfort his mother just before she died in Ireland. He knew he couldn't make the long journey back himself, so instead he sent this verse to remind her of the constant love of Christ.

Just before Joseph's own death, a friend found the lines in his room and asked who wrote it. Joseph's reply was, "The Lord and I did it together."

A few years later, the world-famous evangelist Ira Sankey came across "What a Friend" and included it in his *Sankey's Gospel Hymn Book*, a copy of which seemed to find a place on most pianos around the world. The rest, as they say, is history!

However hidden and unrecognized our actions and efforts may feel at the time, it's surprising how often they are discovered and appreciated by people we might never even know. The simplicity of Joseph's words, drawn from his experience of lost earthly love alongside his deep knowledge of the loving presence of God, has touched the hearts of so many who struggle with their own loss and hurt. There is infinite comfort and reassurance in these verses which all ring with the most obvious solution to our troubles. Take it to the Lord in prayer! So let's do that now…

Are we weak and heavy-laden,
Cumbered with a load of care?
Precious Saviour, still our refuge –
Take it to the Lord in prayer.
Do your friends despise, forsake you?
Take it to the Lord in prayer:
In his arms he'll take and shield you,
You will find a solace there.

A M E N

Saved by Grace

Some day the silver cord will break,
And I no more as now shall sing;
But O the joy when I shall wake
Within the palace of the King!

And I shall see him face to face,
And tell the story, saved by grace;
And I shall see him face to face,
And tell the story, saved by grace.

(Fanny Crosby: 1820–1915)

*F*anny Crosby was a truly remarkable woman. She was just few weeks old when a bad cold caused her eyes to become inflamed. A local doctor treated her by applying hot mustard poultices to her eyes. The immediate and tragic consequence was that she lost her sight completely – but she came to look on her blindness as a blessing, so that when she was only eight years old she was able to write one of her first poems:

Oh, what a happy child I am,
Although I cannot see!
I am resolved that in this world
Contented I will be.

By the time she died, in her nineties, Fanny had written
something like 9,000 hymn texts, sometimes two or three
a day. She became very famous, especially as some of her
most well-known hymns, such as "Blessed Assurance"
and "To God Be the Glory", became favourites of the
international evangelists Dwight Moody and Ira Sankey.
They encouraged thousands to sing them at their rallies
across the United States and elsewhere in the world,
including Great Britain.

Of all her hymns, "Saved by Grace" was the one
she called her "heart song". It was apparently inspired by
words spoken by a pastor friend in his dying breath:

If each of us is faithful to the grace which is given
us by Christ, that same grace which teaches us
how to live will also teach us how to die.

Fanny lived every minute of her life to the full. When,
in her later years, someone suggested that it was a pity
God had denied her sight when she had otherwise been
so blessed, she replied that if she'd been able to make
one request when she was born, it would have been for
blindness – because the very first face she would ever

see would be that of God when she was finally called to heaven.

We are all born with a range of abilities and limitations which we develop and use throughout life in order to become the person others recognize us to be. We are blessed with an array of talents. We might be able to sing or draw. We may be skilful with numbers or writing. Perhaps our appearance and sense of style might draw admiration – or our confidence and qualities of leadership. On the other hand, we are all acutely aware of our shortcomings. In our own minds, we're too fat or too dowdy, too tall, too short, too clumsy, or too slow. Mostly, other people see us much more positively than we imagine ourselves. Physical limitations – such as not being able to see, hear, or move like everyone else – can undermine our sense of worth and purpose.

But if we believe our individual qualities and gifts come from God, then he must have meant us to be exactly as we are. We are taught to use our talents to the best of our ability for the benefit of others. God knows what might hold us back, and he also knows what our capabilities are. Like Fanny Crosby, we might find we have to accept and work round whatever we aren't able to do by making more of the abilities we *do* have. That way, we can become everything God always intended us to be.

Father, you made us and know us better than we know ourselves. Give us courage to face what we feel we can't do, strength to make the most of all we can do, and peace to accept what we simply aren't and never will be. May we never cease to be thankful for all your blessings and gifts to us.

AMEN

Great is Thy Faithfulness

Great is thy faithfulness, O God my Father,
There is no shadow of turning with thee;
Thou changest not, thy compassions, they fail not;
As thou hast been thou for ever wilt be.

Great is thy faithfulness, great is thy faithfulness,
Morning by morning new mercies I see;
All I have needed thy hand hath provided,
Great is thy faithfulness, Lord, unto me.

(Thomas O. Chisholm: 1866–1960)

When you have a tough start in life, it's difficult to imagine how you might make your mark. Thomas Obadiah Chisholm had the most lowly of starts: he was born in a log cabin in Franklin, Kentucky, to a family he spoke of as "dirt poor". His only education came from the little country school where his learning was elementary, to say the most, but his thirst for knowledge stood him in good stead because at the age of sixteen, he was made a teacher in the same school without ever leaving it.

Any Christian education Thomas had until then was plainly lost on him, because it wasn't until he was twenty-eight that he finally found faith made sense to him. That led him to move across Kentucky to Louisville to take on the editorship of *The Pentecostal Herald*. Going into ministry was an easy step from there, and in 1903 he was ordained a Methodist minister with a congregation in another Kentucky town, Scottsville.

Thomas had never been a physically strong man, and before long the sheer hard work needed to serve his congregation became more than he could endure. Before the end of his first year, he moved his family to Indiana where he took up what was to become his life's career as an insurance salesman. So, selling insurance became his job – but his heart and soul were devoted to hymn writing. This man, who described himself as "just an old shoe", went on to write more than 1,200 poems and texts. When trying to explain his passion and purpose, he said, "I have greatly desired that each hymn or poem might have some definite message to the hearts for whom it was written."

There's no doubt that they have, especially in the case of "Great is Thy Faithfulness", which he based on one of his favourite lines from Lamentations (3:22–23):

Great is Thy Faithfulness

*Because of the Lord's great love we are not
consumed, for his compassions never fail. They
are new every morning; great is your faithfulness.*

We are often moved by special moments in our lives when
we feel very keenly God's presence and goodness. At
moments like that, we might find ourselves thanking God
with the words of this song. Thomas, though, said that he
wasn't prompted by one shining moment of gratitude, but
by an ongoing sense of amazement that every morning he
was reassured of the faithfulness of God. He felt that God's
constant care had brought him through many bad times,
such as when money was sparse and his health poor.

We all have periods in our lives when troubles seem
to weigh us down. At the time, we feel isolated, desperate,
and uncertain where to turn. So often, though, with the
benefit of hindsight we are able to see that, although in
our confusion we may have lost sight of God, he never
left our side. Thomas certainly came to that conclusion
throughout his long life – and he was ninety-three years
old when he died in 1960. Throughout it all – from his
humble beginning, through his struggle for a proper
education, his attempt to be a minister, and his constant
health problems – he felt that God not only heard his
prayers but also answered them according to his own
will. God's faithful presence gave Thomas courage, hope,
and purpose.

Love So Amazing

*Father, sometimes life overwhelms us. We feel
swamped, inadequate and without direction. Help us
to remember that you are with us in those dark times
with the same compassion and understanding with
which you encourage us always. May we never cease
to be thankful for your faithfulness to us – and devote
all we are to being steadfast and faithful to you.*

AMEN

And Can It Be

And can it be that I should gain
An interest in the Saviour's blood?
Died he for me, who caused his pain;
For me, who him to death pursued?
Amazing love! How can it be
That thou, my God, shouldst die for me?

(Charles Wesley: 1707–88)

What wonderful people Charles Wesley and his brother John must have been – fascinating, tireless, imaginative, inspiring, and relentless in their mission to tell the world about their belief in the saving power of Christ by faith. The Methodist Church they established has brought understanding and vision to generations of Christians around the world.

John was the main preacher and organizer of the brothers' work, while Charles poured out his new-found understanding of a personal relationship with God in the form of hymn verses. He wrote nearly 9,000 religious poems, of which more than 6,000 can properly be classified as hymns.

John didn't always approve of his brother's writing, which is why he checked each new hymn before it was used. He was pleased to see that Charles displayed his wide and detailed knowledge of the Bible by hinting at biblical quotations in almost every line of verse. What didn't please him as much was the way Charles slipped into writing very personally, which certainly wasn't the style of the day. The words "I" and "me" are peppered throughout much of his work, because Charles came to think of God not only as the ruler of heaven and earth, but also as his personal friend and comforter who knew and understood him completely, accepting his limitations and failings, but loving him still. Through his hymns, Charles comes across as a very *human* being – emotional, loving, excited, overwhelmed, and fulfilled in equal measure in his praise and gratefulness to God. Those qualities, and the enthusiasm with which they are conveyed, speak down the years from one very human man to all of us who find ourselves relating to him in our own experiences of blessings and challenges in our equally human lives.

In fact, their lives must have been more of a challenge than we can possibly imagine. It's estimated that the brothers travelled almost 250,000 miles, sometimes preaching three sermons a day, usually in town squares or fields as huge crowds flocked to hear them. They most certainly weren't always welcome, though. Both brothers were actually ordained ministers of the Anglican Church, but their message was too evangelistic for the church at that time. They were often met with sticks, stones, and insults, and sometimes had to flee from mobs trying to run them out of town. How many of us could stand years of such physical hardship and personal insult without our faith faltering just a little? But the harder the opposition, the more determined the brothers were – and the more inspirational and glorious Charles' hymn writing became.

There are so many lines in this particular hymn that are indelible in our minds, full of wonder at what Christ's life and death means to each and every one of us:

> *Amazing love! How can it be*
> *That thou, my God shouldst die for me?*

In two short lines, Charles has succinctly put into words the full glory of God's gift to us in Christ.

And whose heart hasn't been roused in a full church in fellowship with others, singing together:

> *My chains fell off, my heart was free,*
> *I rose, went forth, and followed thee!*

The Wesley brothers most certainly rose, went forth, and followed God, in spite of the exhaustion, difficulties, and animosity they faced every day. What kept them going was their conviction that God was walking with them as they took the vital truth of his promise made in Christ to all who needed to hear it. And more than three centuries later, we're still hearing that message through the teaching and great hymns which are the legacy of these two remarkable men.

Please bless me, Lord, with the words, the opportunity, and the courage to tell others of your power and presence so that their hearts, too, can be filled with knowledge and love of you.

AMEN

For All the Saints

For all the saints who from their labours rest,
Who thee by faith before the world confessed,
Thy name, O Jesu, be for ever blest.
Alleluia! Alleluia!

(William Walsham How: 1823–97)

I have an image of all those saints from long ago whose lives were totally devoted to God, and I must say I find myself rather daunted by them. They turned their backs on any sense of comfort and left their families, their professions, and often the company of anyone else at all, in order to live in pure and humble poverty. Some lived as hermits, cut off completely from the world. Others travelled the length and breadth of the country to spread the Christian message, often to be faced by violent resistance. Many met an untimely end in the most horrific way as they sacrificed their lives for their faith. Knowing all that, however devoted *we* are to God, I don't much fancy being a saint, do you?

But, to be a saint, does life always have to be so

relentlessly difficult? The writer of this hymn, William Walsham How, was definitely thought of as a bit of a saint by many – including Queen Victoria, who made him the Bishop responsible for the East End of London, which was then a poverty-stricken area in which living conditions were basic, to say the least. William shunned the offer of a fine house and carriage fit for a bishop, choosing instead to live among the poor, taking the bus to get around, just as his parishioners did – and they loved him for it. He especially felt the need to help and minister to children, as he saw them as the hope of tomorrow. He was said to appreciate the simple things in life – simple trust, simple character, simple childhood – and his own lifestyle was frugal and unpretentious, reflecting his deeply humble, reverent faith.

Perhaps William, in his down-to-earth way, helps us to understand how we can be inspired rather than daunted by the saints whose stories of self-sacrifice we've heard all our lives. Perhaps we don't have to turn our backs on present-day comforts, the life we know, or the people we love in order to make a stand for the gospel of Christ. After all, I think God made each one of us unique and individual, and blessed with life in abundance. He knows us as we are, warts and all, and he knows that sometimes we'll stumble and fall. He knows we need his forgiveness, guidance, and protection – but he also understands, better than we ever could, the value of the gifts he's given us, and how we might use them not just for ourselves, but first and foremost for other people. I believe he wants us to become everything he planned for us to be, to show in some small way the steadfastness and trust we admire so much in the great saints.

There are many who excel at doing this. I think the real saints of today live down the road from me and from you. They're the people who suffer from constant chronic pain yet always want to know how *you* are; the soldier who marches off to fight for his country; the dad who works all hours to keep food on the table; the mum who nurses her sick child even though she's exhausted herself; the daughter who lets life pass her by as she cares for the parent she loves. These Christlike qualities of perseverance, acceptance, and courage are often overlooked and undervalued – and yet these are the unsung saints who quietly, constantly, put others' needs before their own.

We feel ordinary and very human, Lord, when we think of the courage and sacrifice of your glorious saints. Give us strength when we feel helpless, direction when we are lost, insight when we see others in pain, and perseverance to support and help all those in need in every way we can. You expect that of us. You gave us the gifts to do your work on earth. We pray for the wisdom and opportunity to use those gifts to your glory.

AMEN

There is a Green Hill Far Away

There is a green hill far away,
Without a city wall,
Where the dear Lord was crucified,
Who died to save us all.

He died that we might be forgiven,
He died to make us good,
That we might go at last to heaven,
Saved by his precious blood.

(Cecil Frances Alexander: 1818–95)

ho doesn't remember singing this hymn when they were in short socks, standing in the school hall during assembly? This is one of the best loved of all children's hymns. It was written by a woman – in spite of her Christian name being *Cecil* – whose passion was to make the stories of the gospel come alive so that children could understand them.

It was probably during her early days as a Sunday School teacher that Frances (as she was mostly known) first thought of using simple poetry as a teaching tool for her pupils to give them a better understanding of the wording of the Creed which they recited in church each Sunday. Hence, "All Things Bright and Beautiful" explained the phrase "Maker of heaven and earth"; "Once in Royal David's City" described "Born of the Virgin Mary", and "There is a Green Hill Far Away" intended to amplify the statement "He suffered under Pontius Pilate, was crucified, died and was buried." By 1848, Frances was able to publish forty-one of her poems in *Hymns for Little Children*, a book which found a place in homes far and wide. It started with a dedication to her own godsons:

> *To my little Godsons, I inscribe these lines hoping*
> *that the language of the verse, which children*
> *love, may help to impress on their minds what*
> *they are, what I have promised for them, and*
> *what they must seek to be.*

Two years later, she married a priest six years younger than herself called William Alexander, and it sounds as if these two enjoyed a marriage in which they shared not only their faith but their sense of humour. Many years later, once William had become Archbishop of Armagh and Primate of all Ireland, he wryly said that he knew he was unlikely to be remembered for any of his achievements in high office, but simply because he was married to the woman who wrote "All Things Bright and Beautiful"!

Many of us as adults owe our basic understanding of the Christian story to hymns written by Frances. Over the years, we may have studied the theology more deeply and have a better perception of the truths of the gospel and what they mean for us and to us – but the simple message of Christ's sacrifice as expressed in this hymn forms the heart of our belief.

Perhaps, from generation to generation, the simplicity of Christ's gift to us has become over-complicated by human interpretation, so that we long to regain our childish sense of thankfulness and wonder as we hear the story of Christ's crucifixion and resurrection. We remember, too, the words of Jesus as we hear them in Matthew 18:2:

> *Unless you change and become like little children,*
> *you will never enter the kingdom of heaven.*

Surely our journey of faith starts with the first step, which accepts that there is a God who created us and loves us unconditionally. After that, we can spend the rest of our lives learning about the nature of God and the gift of his Son on earth. We can experience for ourselves the presence of the Holy Spirit and witness the way in which he touches and changes lives. Our understanding of the power of God grows within us daily through experience and prayer – but a lifetime of faith will still leave us with so many questions, as we want to understand more fully in a way that will only be answered when we join God in heaven. As God's children, we must never stop seeking to learn, and longing for his guidance.

> *O dearly, dearly has he loved,*
> *And we must love him too,*
> *And trust in his redeeming blood,*
> *and try his works to do.*

AMEN

In Christ Alone

In Christ alone my hope is found,
He is my light, my strength, my song;
This Cornerstone, this solid Ground,
Firm through the fiercest drought and storm.
What heights of love, what depths of peace,
When fears are stilled, when strivings cease!
My Comforter, my All in All,
Here in the love of Christ I stand.

(Stuart Townend b. 1963 and Keith Getty b. 1974)

When *Songs of Praise* recently organized a poll to find the most popular hymn in the UK, I wondered for the first time in all the years I've been presenting the programme whether "How Great Thou Art", the perennial favourite which has been top of the poll for as long as anyone can remember, might be pipped to the winning post by the haunting, inspirational, classically beautiful worship song, "In Christ Alone". In the end it was a tight-run race, and the old favourite took the crown as the hymn congregations most love to sing – but I think the runner-up, "In Christ Alone", which tells the complete story of Christ's life, death, and resurrection in its four short verses, embeds itself in our hearts and sings in our soul. But then, Stuart Townend and Keith Getty have a truly inspirational way of weaving words and music into worship which is easy and accessible for us all. Like the old masters, their thoughts are theologically sound and ring with truth and vision – but they bring that truth to us couched in beautiful modern melodies which help us think afresh about what we've always believed.

Certainly, these words ring with reassurance – in Christ we find hope, strength, love, peace, and comfort, because to him we are known and cherished as the flawed, complex individuals we all are. We can turn to him when life's challenges threaten to overwhelm us and we feel fearful and inadequate. In the vastness of his love and the might of his majesty, we are told that *nothing can ever pluck me from his hand* – our God who created the universe and changed the whole of history, and yet still longs for the deepest of relationships with each one of us. We struggle to prove our worth, and we pin our hopes on how well we're doing and how devoted we are to the Christian life, when the truth is that success or failure in what *we* do means little compared to the infinite gift of what Christ has done for us.

One very moving message came from a young American soldier serving in Iraq who sang and reflected on each of these verses whenever he could:

We are losing soldiers here every day. The promise that I am his and knowing that he is mine brings him incredibly close to me. As I drive with my M-16 pointed out the window and my 9mm pistol tucked in my flak jacket pocket, I can tell you that I feel more secure in claiming the promise no power of hell, no scheme of man can ever pluck me from his hand than I do with that rifle or pistol.

Usually this hymn starts very quietly and prayerfully and builds to a triumphant crescendo which gets people to their feet as they are fired up with praise and thankfulness for God's gift and promise to us in Christ. So our prayer today is the last verse of this hymn. It can be sung along with others at the top of your voice with your arms raised – or thought through and whispered, with your head bowed, your mind full of wonder, and your hands clasped in prayer.

No guilt in life, no fear in death,
This is the power of Christ in me;
From life's first cry to final breath,
Jesus commands my destiny.

In Christ Alone

No power of hell, no scheme of man,
Can ever pluck me from his hand;
Till he returns or calls me home,
Here in the power of Christ I'll stand.

Amen

It is Well with My Soul

When peace, like a river, attendeth my way,
When sorrows like sea billows roll;
Whatever my lot, thou has taught me to say,
It is well, it is well, with my soul.
It is well, with my soul,
It is well, with my soul,
It is well, it is well, with my soul.

(Horatio Spafford: 1828–88)

*I*t's shocking how quickly comfortable life can turn into a nightmare. In 1870, lawyer and church elder Horatio Spafford and his wife Anna were an affluent couple with extensive real estate along the shore of Lake Michigan, when their contentment was shattered by the loss of their four-year-old son from scarlet fever. The following year, the Great Chicago Fire destroyed all their properties. To ease his wife's deep depression and lift the spirits of his four daughters, Horatio arranged for them all to take a trip to Europe in November 1873. On the day they were due to leave, Horatio was faced with a sudden business emergency, so he sent Anna and the family on ahead with the plan that he would follow a few days later. In the middle of the Atlantic Ocean, their steamer was struck by a British iron sailing ship and sank within twelve minutes. Out of 307 passengers, only eighty-one were rescued, one of them being Anna Spafford.

Anna spoke later of how she remembered being sucked violently downwards when her baby Tanetta was ripped from her arms by heavy debris. Their older daughters, Maggie and Annie, clung to a piece of wood for almost an hour before they wearily lost their grip and floated away to their death. Their younger sister, Bessie, was never seen or found.

When Anna finally reached Cardiff, she sent Horatio a telegram with a brief and heartbreaking message, "Saved alone." Horatio immediately set sail on another ship to bring his wife home. Several days later he was called to the bridge by the captain when the ship passed the place where it was reckoned the tragic steamer had gone down. That night, alone in his cabin, with a faith that never faltered, Horatio penned the words of this moving hymn. Later he wrote to Anna's sister:

> *On Thursday last we passed over the spot where she went down, in mid-ocean, the waters three miles deep. But I do not think of our dear ones there. They are safe, folded, the dear lambs.*

Who among us, faced with such dreadful tragedy, could write words like these, not just of acceptance and deep faith, but of thanks, hope, and praise? To add to the couple's despair, some of their Christian community back in Chicago started talking about the accident as if it were some sort of punishment from God! Believing without doubt that God was good and that he would see his daughters again in heaven, Horatio and the family, including the two other young daughters they'd been blessed with, finally fulfilled their lifelong wish to live in Jerusalem. In the old part of the city they established The American Colony to bring both practical help and the love of Jesus to the needy, sick, and homeless. Their own loss gave them deeper compassion for the suffering of others, and they proved so inspirational that their work and legacy continues in The Spafford Children's Centre in Jerusalem to this very day.

Horatio and Anna believed that God's hand was in everything that happened to them and their family, and although the loss of their beloved daughters and little son broke their hearts, they trusted that, through God, all would be well. Their faith came through triumphant and strong, and Horatio's generous, faithful, remarkable verses have since brought comfort to so many who suffer loss and pain.

It is Well with My Soul

*When tragedy strikes and we're faced with the shock
of unexpected loss, we can lose sight of you in the
depths of our despair. Help us, Comforter Lord, to
sense your presence in the darkness of our hurt and
confusion. Draw us close and help us to find the
strength to reflect the compassionate love you show us
to others who are struggling and in pain.*

AMEN

Make Me a Channel
of Your Peace

Make me a channel of your peace.
Where there is hatred let me bring your love;
Where there is injury, your pardon, Lord;
And where there's doubt, true faith in you.

(Prayer of St Francis: 1181–1226, by Sebastian Temple: 1928–97)

*T*hese words are said to have been inspired by Francis, the humble saint who dedicated himself as a channel of God's peace when he gave up an affluent lifestyle in twelfth-century Italy to live in poverty among the sick, desperate, and most needy people in the land – a way of life followed ever since by the Franciscan Order established in his name.

To be a channel for God's peace! Most sincere Christians would pray to be used in this way, especially when we hear of remarkable people who have heard God's call and responded by putting their lives, their security, their homes, and their reputations on the line in order to follow what they believe to be God's will. Could we ever do that?

One man I'll never forget was well into his eighties when I met him. He'd had a successful career in industry but, sadly, just at the point he retired, his wife died. He was left in an empty house and for some time he rattled around, feeling he was too old to be useful to anyone. Then he discovered the work of the Peace Corps which promotes world peace and friendship. Much to the concern of his family and friends, he set off to become an International Peace Observer. This meant he would stand in war zones where confrontation and anger was at its most dangerous, and simply observe what was going on, quietly writing down what he saw and heard. This is a powerful tool which can feel very threatening to those who are bullying others during conflict. It's surprising how the quiet, impartial presence of an observer can make aggressors step back from the brink.

This man had paid many times for his bravery. He'd been threatened with guns and knocked to the ground on several occasions. I asked him why, at his age, he didn't just put his feet up and enjoy a well-deserved rest? He said that as he had no fear whatsoever of death, threats of physical harm meant little to him. What he dreaded more was the thought that he would die in his bed, no longer of use to anyone, especially God.

His courage takes my breath away. Most of us wouldn't feel able to make such a dramatic gesture – but perhaps, in our own way, we can allow our lives to be used for God's purpose. That means acknowledging his will before our own, looking for what is just and compassionate rather than simply doing what feels right for us. It means listening to what others are saying rather than just expecting them to listen to us. It means not always demanding what we feel is rightfully ours, but considering first of all what we can give to others who are hurting or in need.

It is no wonder these words were part of the morning prayers of Mother Teresa every day at the Missionaries of Charity in Calcutta, or that Archbishop Desmond Tutu quoted them as he accepted the 1984 Nobel Peace Prize. We may not win prizes or change the world, but in our own small corner, allowing God's love to work through us can help to create his kingdom on earth.

Make me a channel of your peace.
Where there's despair in life, let me bring hope;
Where there is darkness, only light;
And where there's sadness, ever joy.

AMEN

For the Beauty of the Earth

For the beauty of the earth,
For the beauty of the skies,
For the love which from our birth
Over and around us lies:

Christ our God, to thee we raise
This our sacrifice of praise.

(F. S. Pierpoint: 1835–1917)

*S*ometimes we don't appreciate what's around us until we move away and miss it. That's what might well have happened to Folliott Sandford Pierpoint (what a great name for a hymn writer!) when he left his home in the elegant town of Bath to begin his studies at Cambridge University in preparation for his life's career as a classics master. In his late twenties he returned to his home near the Avon valley, and almost immediately wrote these wonderful words.

When we were making a *Songs of Praise* programme from Bath some years ago, I was taken to the spot overlooking that valley where it is said Folliott was standing when he was moved to put pen to paper. What lay before me was a scene of rolling hills interspersed with trees and hedgerows, with lush grassland tumbling down towards the River Avon. The view simply took my breath away, just as it had Folliott's way back in the 1860s.

But this hymn isn't simply an outpouring of praise for God's glorious creation. I wonder whether Folliott hadn't quite realized how much he had missed and now really valued his life at home, because the following verses are full of other reasons for which he wanted to give thanks. He considered the intricate and awe-inspiring design of his own body, and saw God's hand in it. He thought about the love of his family and friends that surrounded him, and marvelled at it. And he cherished the fellowship of his church and the divine gifts it brought him. It was as if the glory of that springtime scene sent him into an ecstasy of appreciation and contentment for all the blessings he saw and sensed around him.

Moments like that can be so healing. When our own life is in disarray, with problems nagging away at our sense of well-being and peace of mind, it's very reassuring to have such a graphic display of God's power and goodness putting everything into perspective. I remember a very dear friend of mine telling me of just such a moment. She came from a farming family, and one of her fondest memories of her father was the impact of the lambing season on the whole family, and the sight of her Dad out in the field with the sheep. During the months of intense bereavement after his death, lambing time came round again, and she told me how she'd shed heartbroken tears at the sight of new lambs in a field where she could picture him so clearly. But something dawned on her as she looked at this familiar scene – the recognition of God's hand in the world around; the constant promise of his presence in the cycle of the seasons, the beauty of the countryside, the produce of the land. As she watched, she found herself filled with a sense of reassurance and confidence that life would go on, and that whatever lay before her, God would be in it with her.

That's not a new thought. Three thousand years ago, a psalmist said, "I will lift up mine eyes unto the hills, from whence cometh my help" (Psalm 121:1, KJV).

So get out your walking boots! There's hope in "dem dere hills"!

How can we doubt you when we see the glory of your gifts wherever we look? From the magnificence of creation to the intimate feeling of a baby's finger curling around ours, or the reassuring thud of our own heartbeat, or the fellowship we find in the company of others, especially when we worship together – your blessings are too many to count! We are humbled and full of thanks for your goodness and love.

AMEN

Nearer, My God, to Thee

Nearer, my God, to Thee, nearer to Thee!
E'en though it be a cross that raiseth me;
Still all my song shall be nearer, my God, to Thee,
Nearer, my God, to Thee, nearer to Thee!

(Sarah Flower Adams: 1805–1848)

When Sarah Adams wrote these words at her home in Loughton, Essex, back in 1841, she could never have imagined that it would become famous for the most tragic of reasons. It's commonly believed that this was the last piece of music played by the band on the *Titanic* when that great liner sank on her maiden voyage in April 1912.

These words came to Sarah after she'd read the story in Genesis 28 of Jacob at Bethel, when he placed his head on a stone to sleep, then dreamt of a ladder reaching up to heaven. Something in that story seemed to touch hearts, because "Nearer, My God, to Thee" had become associated with the journey towards heaven made after death on several memorable occasions before that fateful night on the *Titanic*. In September 1901, when American President William McKinley died with the lines of the first verse on his lips, hundreds of bands across the United States played the hymn in his memory. And in 1906, it was apparently sung by the doomed crew and passengers of the SS *Valencia* as it sank off the Canadian coast.

Several people who survived the sinking of the *Titanic* spoke of how, when the ship first hit the iceberg, band leader Wallace Hartley led his musicians in a jaunty selection of music aimed at calming the passengers. Dance music and comic songs did little, however, to stop the increasing panic as passengers began to realize they were facing probable death, so, as a devout Methodist, he started to play hymns. "Nearer, My God, to Thee", with its reassuring vision of welcome and rest in heaven, was the hymn requested by many as they faced the awful reality of death for themselves and their families. Out of 2,223 people who sailed out from Southampton on that voyage, 1,517 lost their lives, including Wallace and his musicians.

Sarah painted a picture of heaven full of angels waiting to welcome "the wanderer" with mercy and love. What comfort there is in that image, because it means we have nothing to fear once death has come, and we draw near to God. What Christians worry about most is not *being* dead, because we believe we will be with God. What we truly fear is the mishap or illness that might be the cause of our death. Will we suffer? Will we be frightened? Will we feel helpless and hopeless? Will we have people who love us at our side, or might we have to face the prospect of death alone? Will our faith suddenly take on a whole new relevance? Will our belief be strong enough to support us through physical deterioration and pain, and calm us as death draws close?

Some years ago, I was fortunate to spend time talking to the remarkable founder of the Hospice Movement, Dame Cicely Saunders, whose life's work was devoted to making the journey towards death as pain-free and fulfilling for the patient and their family as it's possible to be. She spoke of enabling people "to live every moment of their lives", and she quoted her husband who, when he was dying, spoke with some excitement of death being "an adventure".

When our physical bodies die, our souls are free to join their Creator, and Christ himself reassured us of the welcome waiting for us there, at the start of John 14:

Do not let your hearts be troubled. Trust in God; trust also in me. In my Father's house are many rooms; if it were not so, I would have told you. I am going there to prepare a place for you. And if I go and prepare a place for you, I will come back and take you to be with me that you also may be where I am.

Nearer, My God, to Thee

Lord God, we long to be near you, both in life and in death. Be with us on the journey, and there at our homecoming.

AMEN

O Love That Wilt Not Let Me Go

O love that wilt not let me go,
I rest my weary soul in thee;
I give thee back the life I owe,
That in thine ocean depths its flow
May richer, fuller be.

(George Matheson: 1842–1906)

*O*f all the hymns I would describe as a "prayer in my pocket", this one is my personal favourite. We all go through patches in life which are tough, distressing, or confusing, and for me, the first two lines of this hymn are a spiritual first-aid kit I often find myself reaching for. Do you know that feeling of utter exhaustion when things seem to be piling up and you're not quite coping? Doesn't the thought of God's love never letting you go, so that you can rest your "weary soul" in his strength and protection, feel like exactly what you need?

Perhaps these words resonate so poignantly with us because their author, Glasgow-born George Matheson, knew very well that feeling of despair. In fact, when asked what prompted him to write them, he said they were "the fruits of suffering, written when I was alone and suffering a mental anguish over something that no one else knew."

We do know he penned this hymn in a matter of minutes on the eve of the wedding of his sister, who had been his housekeeper and carer for most of his life. To lose that care would be devastating for George as he'd known since a young boy that he had an incurable condition which would render him completely blind in adulthood. The illness hadn't stopped him graduating with a first-class honours degree when he was nineteen – or sharing the experience of many young men in finding the love of his life among his fellow students while at university. They were in love; they planned to marry – until his fiancée was told that George would spend most of his life as a blind man. That was too much for her. She broke off their engagement, and broke his heart.

That disappointment in human love seemed to spur him on to an even greater appreciation of the unfailing love of God. He became so popular as a preacher at Innellan on the Clyde that Queen Victoria herself arranged to listen to him, and was plainly moved by his prayerful compassion for those struggling with the ups and downs of life, whether physical, practical, or emotional. It was through his own life challenges that George learned what he was really made of, and he came to appreciate that, even if his blindness was a limitation in some ways, he was able to excel in others. God had given him a unique set of talents and qualities which allowed him to be an encouraging and inspirational support to others in need.

Sometimes, the talents we've been given don't seem to balance out our limitations, or provide us with the ability we feel we need to face life's many challenges. God knows better, though. He knows what we're capable of, and he is alongside us through both the good times and the difficult. George Matheson was able to look back and realize that it was through the tough patches, when he could do nothing more than place his trust in God, that his faith was tested and his true character forged.

Our prayer is the third verse of this hymn, the one I love most, because it speaks of promise and future contentment in that unforgettable and illuminating line about tracing "the rainbow through the rain". Whatever dark clouds may be gathering around you at the moment, take comfort from the encouragement of these words:

> *O joy that seekest me through pain,*
> *I cannot close my heart to thee;*
> *I trace the rainbow through the rain,*
> *And feel the promise is not vain*
> *That morn shall tearless be.*

AMEN

Stand Up, Stand Up for Jesus

Stand up, stand up for Jesus,
Ye soldiers of the cross!
Lift high his royal banner,
It must not suffer loss.
From victory unto victory
His army he shall lead,
Till every foe is vanquished
And Christ is Lord indeed.

(George Duffield: 1818–88)

I remember this hymn very clearly from school assemblies where we changed the first two lines to sing, "Sit down, sit down for Jesus, The people at the back can't see" – except that the word "people" was replaced by something a bit more colourful! Was I a teenage hoodlum to do that – or have generations of schoolchildren sung exactly the same thing? Perhaps if we'd known the tragic story that prompted these words, we'd have shown a bit more respect.

The story is not about the hymn writer, George Duffield, but his friend and fellow pastor, Dudley Tyng, a young man with very strong and outspoken views. He bravely denounced slavery as "immoral and unchristian", then made clear his belief that all men are sinners by nature who need to repent if they are ever to enter heaven. The rich and fashionable congregation he served in Philadelphia soon decided he should leave, so he moved his wife and boys to a family farm outside the city, and set up his own Church of the Covenant. When he also began speaking at the Philadelphia YMCA, people were drawn to this charismatic preacher, first in their hundreds and then in their thousands. At Jayne's Hall in March 1858, more than 5,000 men came along to hear him say during his address, "I would rather this right arm were amputated at the trunk than I should come short of my duty in delivering God's message."

How prophetic those words became because, the following week, as he watched his mule driving a grain-shelling machine at the farm, his sleeve caught in the cogs and dragged his arm into the machinery. In an attempt to save his life, doctors amputated the limb at the shoulder, but the loss of blood and physical trauma were terminal. As George Duffield and other friends gathered around Dudley's deathbed, they asked him if he wanted to say anything to encourage his followers.

"Tell them," whispered the dying man, "to stand up

for Jesus."

Those words touched George deeply because, before he preached to his own congregation a few days later, he'd written the words of this hymn. It soon became a great favourite, not just with churchgoers, but also among the soldiers of the Civil War who sang it as they marched.

These words aren't about worldly battles, though. They're based on the warning we find in Ephesians 6 that our lives in Christ are a fight for faith in the midst of spiritual enemies. God calls us to stand in the strength he provides.

Many of us live in comfortable, open-minded countries where being a Christian is readily accepted. Millions of Christians in other parts of the world practise their faith in the face of cruel, tormenting persecution, even to death. Whereas our faith is rarely tested, for them, standing up for Christ might put not just them, but also their families, in grave danger. Would we, challenged by that sort of physical threat, be brave enough to stand up for Jesus? Are we even prepared to stand up in our own country when we know the Christian message needs to be heard loud and clear? Do we speak out when we feel our Christian principles are being compromised, or our beliefs undermined? Do we make sure we're "delivering God's message", perhaps not to crowds of thousands as Dudley did, but in our own way to our children, friends, and communities?

Let's pray for God's help as we commit ourselves to standing up for Christ:

Father, we think of the saints who have been persecuted to death for love of Christ, and are humbled by the depth of their faith and commitment. Fill us with courage, strengthen our resolve, and give us the words we need to spread the message of your gospel to a world that needs to hear now, more than ever before.

AMEN

Forgive Our Sins

Forgive our sins, as we forgive,
You taught us, Lord, to pray;
But you alone can grant us grace
To live the words we say.

How can your pardon reach and bless
The unforgiving heart
That broods on wrongs, and will not let
Old bitterness depart?

(Rosamond Herklots: 1905–87)

There is so much poignancy in these words. Don't we all know people who find it impossible to let old grievances go? How many of us live with rifts between family members which have lasted so long that no one can quite remember *why* they're not speaking to each other? For everyone except the people involved, the detail of the argument probably faded long ago, leaving just a general sense of sadness that life should be wasted on resentments that are so woefully pointless.

Because each of us is an individual with our own set of priorities and opinions, it's inevitable that we'll sometimes clash with those around us. Honest discussion about different viewpoints can be both enlightening and constructive. We're inclined to be creatures of habit, always thinking and doing what we've always thought and done, but sometimes a fresh pair of eyes might see things in a completely different way. I remember my teenage son, Max, stopping me in my tracks on more than one occasion when he challenged me to explain why I insisted that certain household routines should never change. Mostly I could explain from long experience what might happen if we didn't do things my way – but sometimes I found myself agreeing with him! It was a good exercise for us both, and he grew up knowing that I respected him enough to listen to his opinion, as long as he valued and respected my opinion too.

Long-term grudges can become ingrained when the people involved have no respect for the opinion of others. They feel they have a monopoly of right which allows them no space to consider *why* another person spoke or acted in the way they did. All too often, there's pride at stake. Someone has acted unjustly against us. Only the most grovelling of apologies will remedy the situation, and a complete capitulation that *our* opinion was right all along. But whenever two people view the same event, their perceptions and reactions to what happened can differ greatly in accordance with their own viewpoint and loyalties. That doesn't make one opinion more valid than the other; it just makes them different – and, in the end, agreeing to differ may be the only way forward.

How often have we heard of siblings who haven't spoken for years meeting up at their mother's funeral, where just seeing each other again in such an emotional setting ends with them hugging each other and wondering why on earth they left it so long?

Jesus taught us a daily prayer in which we say, "Forgive us our sins as we forgive those who sin against us." The first part of that instruction is something we can only mean if we accept that we do sometimes put our own wishes before the wishes of others, resulting in great harm or pain. Acknowledging that we *all* need forgiveness is the first step.

The harder challenge, though, is to recognize that because everyone is individual in personality, ability, and background, they may sometimes act or speak in a way which offends or hurts us. Christ asks us to forgive them, just as we ask him to forgive us when we cause hurt by our words or actions. Unless we do, the feeling of resentment and injustice festers away at the very heart of us, clouding our judgment, souring our relationships, and overshadowing any hope of peace and well-being not just in our own lives, but also in the lives of those who love and live with us.

Sometimes people can be selfish and thoughtless. Please, Lord, don't let that be me! If so, I am truly sorry and ask for forgiveness. And I humbly ask you to help me to let go of my resentment towards those who've offended me, and find your forgiveness in my heart.

AMEN

Count Your Blessings

When upon life's billows you are tempest tossed,
When you are discouraged, thinking all is lost,
Count your many blessings, name them one by
*   one*
And it will surprise you what the Lord hath done.

(Johnson Oatman, Jr: 1856–1922)

When following in the footsteps of a father who has a wonderful talent, it can sometimes take a while for a son to find his own chance to shine. Johnson Oatman grew up in Lumbertown, New Jersey, where his father's rich, powerful voice was recognized as the best in the state. Young Johnson tried hard to live up to his family's expectations, working first as a junior member of the family business before recognizing a sense of calling to become a minister in the Methodist Church. Even when he was ordained, he was restless in just one church, so he went around preaching wherever and whenever he could, still not yet feeling that he'd found his true path in life.

It wasn't until he was thirty-six that he discovered his own outstanding talent. Having decided that he would never be able to sing like his father, he thought he'd have a go at writing hymns which others could sing. He imagined them becoming so popular that he could preach to millions through them.

He wasn't far wrong. He started writing in 1897, and by the time he died in 1922 he had written more than 5,000 hymn texts. Many of them are still very familiar, but none more so than this one, "Count Your Blessings".

Would you say you "count your blessings"? Or is your life so full of all kinds of difficulties and stress that you're too busy worrying to have time for much of that! We *all* worry – and although our individual circumstances are unique, our feelings are probably very much the same. We worry about family issues, money problems, the challenge of illness, how long we'll be able to continue working – or perhaps whether we'll ever actually get a job at all. Those personal problems may well keep us awake at night – but they're just the tip of the iceberg, because we have so many global issues to worry about, too! We think about the friction and lack of understanding that pits one country or tradition against another, and wonder if our children are likely to have to suffer war as a result of what we see brewing now. We worry about pollution and climate change and violence. We mourn the lack of neighbourliness that generally seems to be absent in our communities nowadays.

What do they say about seeing life as a glass half empty or half full? We can choose to live in a permanent state of depression, or we can take a good look at all the wonderful blessings that are simply ours – the people we love, the things we cherish, the talents we enjoy, the pleasures available to us in the beauty of the world around us. Often it's the simple things that mean the most – the warmth of our child's hug, an arm around our shoulders when we need it most, a reassuring word of encouragement that spurs us on. They can't ever take away the challenges we face, the limitations we have to accept, the pain we bear, or the fear we sometimes feel – but they are small reassurances from God that he is in the struggle with us, knowing our worries, sharing our concerns.

Father, sometimes we are so consumed by what we think we haven't got, cannot do, and may not have that we overlook the myriad wonderful ways in which you have already blessed us. Even when worries seem to overwhelm us, we pray that you'll open our eyes to all the ways in which you provide everything we truly need. More than anything, what we need most is faith and trust in you.

AMEN

Dear Lord and Father of Mankind

Dear Lord and Father of mankind,
Forgive our foolish ways!
Reclothe us in our rightful mind;
In purer lives thy service find,
In deeper reverence, praise.

Breathe through the heats of our desire
Thy coolness and thy balm;
Let flesh be dumb, let flesh retire;
Speak through the earthquake, wind and fire,
O still, small voice of calm!

(John Greenleaf Whittier: 1807–92)

*T*his is such a dearly loved hymn. I've sung it as part of congregations of hundreds in glorious cathedrals where the music sweeps across walls steeped in history. I've sung it along with handfuls of others in small village churches where the beauty of the words bound us together in worship. Most memorably of all, I sang it along with the other pilgrims who'd been my companions during a trip to the Holy Land. We sat on traditional wooden boats in the middle of the Sea of Galilee where we could so easily picture Christ walking on water to be with us, or asleep at the stern while a storm raged around the terrified disciples. The veil between heaven and earth seemed very thin there. We felt the presence of God so keenly that none of us needed to *see* Christ on our boat to *know* he was with us.

John Greenleaf Whittier would have loved that moment on Galilee and the prayerful atmosphere his words created. He was a Quaker and had been brought up on a New England farm in a community where praising God was a way of life. However, in the Quaker tradition, worship was always in silence, and John himself had a strong dislike of highly emotional religion. He believed that God could best be found in quiet stillness, where it may be possible to hear that "still, small voice of calm" which he mentions in the last line of this hymn.

In fact, he didn't write a "hymn" at all, but a very long poem warning against the dangers of "The Brewing of Soma". Soma was an intoxicating drink made from a fungus, and was used by some Hindus in India to produce a hallucinogenic effect which led to a state of religious frenzy. Not for the same reason, perhaps, but isn't that a bit like some of the substances taken by drug-takers of all ages and backgrounds in our own communities nowadays? John was appalled that such inappropriate "aids" should be considered necessary, especially during religious gatherings, when he knew any sincere worshipper could find God simply through inward peace and prayer.

In the familiar verses of this hymn, John talks about "our foolish ways" and our need to ask for forgiveness – and most of us know all too well how much that need is with us day by day. He also talks about how we should seek God "in purer lives" and "deeper reverence", and "in the beauty of thy peace" find that "strain and stress" are lifted from our souls. What a wonderful, reassuring thought! And dotted throughout the lines are words like *simple, gracious, silence, hush, noiseless, quietness, coolness,* and *balm* – all gently suggesting that the way to subdue the clutter and busyness of our lives is through peace and calm. That's how we can finally hear the "still, small voice" of God which brings sense and comfort to the materialistic bustle of our lives.

I'd like to think that John would finally approve of his words being set to Sir Hubert Parry's haunting melody "Repton", because the two seem to fit like a glove. And in spite of the soaring beauty of that melody, the last line is always finished quietly, like a heartfelt prayer. This hymn *is* a prayer, one which is indelibly lodged in our minds for us to sing or whisper to ourselves whenever we feel life is becoming too frantic and stressful.

> *Drop thy still dews of quietness,*
> *Till all our strivings cease;*
> *Take from our souls the strain and stress,*
> *And let our ordered lives confess*
> *The beauty of thy peace.*

A M E N

Jesus Bids Us Shine

Jesus bids us shine with a pure, clear light,
Like a little candle burning in the night.
In this world is darkness; so we must shine,
You in your small corner, and I in mine.

(Susan Warner: 1819–85)

The cadets at West Point Military Academy were in for a regular treat in the mid 1800s once talented sisters Susan Warner and Anna Bartlett Warner moved with their family into a large old farmhouse on Constitution Island in the Hudson River. Every Sunday afternoon, the ladies would send a servant to bring the cadets from the Military Academy to their home on the island where the young gentlemen could take part in Bible classes, followed by tea and gingerbread. Not only were both sisters highly successful and popular novel writers, but they also shared a love of hymn writing, often helping each other with inspiration. Anna is said to have written most of the dearly loved children's hymn,

"Jesus Loves Me, This I Know", and Susan is credited with the success of the equally popular "Jesus Bids Us Shine", both of which became Sunday School favourites around the world.

These are words learned in childhood but never forgotten, especially my favourite line, "You in your small corner, and I in mine". What a lovely image that conjures up, of each of us spreading a little Christian light into the dark world in whatever corner is ours! The problem is that often our little circles of light don't shine brightly enough, perhaps because we can easily feel that our own patch is all that matters to us as we don't have any influence further afield. It's much easier to blame others for the ills we see in the world around us – the politicians, the financiers, the leaders who need to take responsibility for nationwide or worldwide problems which are plainly beyond our limited control.

We've all done it, haven't we – complained that *they* should do this and *they* haven't done that – but who exactly do we think *they* are? Well, *they* are just people like us – and it's definitely going to take a joint effort if we really want to see change for the better. As Christians, whatever walk of life we're in, we must be prepared to do our bit to bring about that change. At Christmas time we all pray for *peace on earth*, yet how many of us are prepared to put ourselves out to do something practical to make God's peace a reality for all?

Through prayer and commitment, we need to start creating that peace within ourselves – in our own hearts, in our prayers, in our relationships and homes, in our communities and towns and cities, in our own country, and in every country across the world. After all, great oak trees from little acorns grow – and if we truly mean to bring about peace on earth, then let our words and actions speak for us as we allow ourselves to become channels of God's love.

Our television screens are full of disturbing news about the injustice, cruelty, bullying, and selfishness which seem to be all around us these days, and it's easy to feel that we are too unimportant and powerless to make a difference. It takes courage to stand up for what we know to be right, but once our voice is raised, we may well find that many others are encouraged to raise their voices too. If we simply do what we can in our own small way to bring peace to others, together we can change the world! Together, we can let God's light shine into the darkest places of hatred, pain, and despair. Together, we can make a difference.

Jesus bids us shine, then, for all around
Many kinds of darkness in the world abound,
Sin and want and sorrow; so we must shine,
You in your small corner, and I in mine.

AMEN

Amazing Grace

Amazing grace! How sweet the sound
That saved a wretch like me;
I once was lost, but now am found,
Was blind, but now I see.

(John Newton: 1725–1807)

It's the word *wretch* in the second line of this moving, evocative hymn that always gets me. There is so much self-loathing in that word, as if this person has reached rock bottom, appalled by themselves and the depths to which they've sunk. We don't need to be slave traders like John Newton, the writer of this hymn, to recognize in ourselves that feeling of being ashamed of our actions and reactions, and completely beyond redemption. But this is a hymn that rings not just of experience, but also of hope and forgiveness. God's grace has changed everything, accepting, enabling, and saving even the gravest sinner.

Mind you, as sinners go, John Newton could tell a tale or two. He went to sea when he was just a boy, and was later press-ganged into the Navy. The rebellious young man clashed with authority and was flogged for desertion, finally ending up in jail. By that time, he only cared about himself, so he had no qualms when he eventually ended up in the most despicable of all trades, as the master of slave ships.

By 21 March 1748 he was still only twenty-three years old, and yet it was a date he would always remember. A raging storm was blowing off the north-west coast of Ireland, and Newton's ship was caught in the midst of it. Thundering waves pounded the helpless vessel again and again, until John and his shipmates felt certain the ship would break into pieces. Without thinking, non-believer John cried out from the heart, "Lord, have mercy on us!" Then another thought struck him: What mercy can there be for me? He bowed his head and prayed for all he was worth.

John and his crew didn't die that night. The storm abated and the ship was saved. More importantly, John was saved as he realized for the first time that the God he'd never believed in had answered his prayer. "On that day," he later wrote, "the Lord sent from on high and delivered me from deep waters."

That was a turning point. Before long, John gave up seafaring to become tide surveyor at Liverpool docks. He began to study theology, Greek, and Hebrew, and finally in 1764 was ordained a Church of England curate and sent to the small town of Olney in Buckinghamshire. This is where he wrote "Amazing Grace" and many other well-known hymns, before moving on to a parish in London where he found himself able to influence government members, including future prime minister William Wilberforce. He died in 1807, nine months after seeing Parliament vote to abolish the slave trade in the British Empire forever.

We all do wrong things. We think, speak, and act wrongly, and sometimes find ourselves so entrenched in a particular set of circumstances that, even if our conscience pricks us, we can't find the will or the strength to stand up and admit how badly we've behaved. It takes courage, searing honesty, and genuine humility, none of which comes easily. Most of us can only find the guidance we need if we open our hearts in prayer. Christ gave his life for our sins, allowing forgiveness and second chances if we truly wish to repent and reform. And once that change is made, great things can happen. Just think of John Newton who made an excellent living out of the misery of innocent slaves, but who later, through faith, became a major force in finally bringing the evil trade to an end.

*Father, forgive our sins. Open our eyes to the pain
we cause others when we don't think, we don't act,
or we do hurtful things which are self-serving and
thoughtless. Give us the strength to change, to stand
up for what we know to be right. Bless us with courage
and resolve always to do the best we can for others –
and for you.*

AMEN

God Moves in a Mysterious Way

God moves in a mysterious way
His wonders to perform;
He plants his footsteps in the sea
And rides upon the storm.

(William Cowper: 1731–1800)

For William Cowper, God was indeed a mystery – but then, life itself was often a complete mystery to him. He suffered from what we would now recognize as clinical depression, which meant that he constantly struggled with mental anguish that pushed him on several occasions to try to take his own life.

It seems that a scar of grief was left on young William's heart when he lost his mother at the age of six, leaving him to be brought up by his father with whom he had such a difficult relationship that he was sent away to boarding school by the time he was ten, where he was cruelly bullied by older boys.

His father decided a career in law was what William needed, which led to years of study followed by nearly a decade in law practice during which he achieved little success. This was because William had such a low opinion of his ability that he felt unworthy to serve others or attract business for himself.

In 1764, during one of his darkest periods of depression, William was confined to the St Albans Insane Asylum – and it was there that he happened upon a Bible on a bench in the garden. That was the start of his conversion to faith, and for the rest of his life he was comforted by the assurance of God's goodness, even though he had great difficulty believing himself worthy of God's love.

Eventually he went to live in the small Buckinghamshire town of Olney where he was looked after by a clergyman's widow, Mrs Unwin, while doing what he could to assist with parish life. In a coincidence which could only have been part of God's plan, William soon met the curate of the parish who happened to be John Newton, the legendary slave-ship captain turned minister and hymn writer. John recognized how depressed and naturally reclusive William was, and as the two men became friends, they would talk for hours as they walked together to visit parishioners, often speaking of their shared love of poetry. Perhaps it was on those walks that they began writing hymns to be sung at their weekly prayer meetings at Olney Church. In 1779, *The Olney Hymnbook* was published, containing hymns written by both men, many of which are still great favourites today.

Nowadays we have a more realistic understanding of depression. We recognize that people can't *just pull themselves together*, as they were so often told to in the past. Their inability to cope with everyday life and the anguish they suffer because of it often requires medical treatment over long periods of time, and undermines confidence, self-worth, and motivation.

Although most of us don't experience the very real symptoms of clinical depression, most of us go through times in life when troubles seem to weigh us down until we sink into a form of depression where we wonder whether anything is worthwhile. Sudden change in a relationship or circumstances, illness, or financial problems can overwhelm us until we can't see a way forward, plummeting us into a pit of fear and exhaustion.

Just like William Cowper, it is at those times, when we are at rock bottom, that we are most likely to find God. When we're on our knees with despair and weariness, God is only ever a prayer away. No skill is required or words needed. Heart to heart, soul to soul, he will hear our cry until we sense his still, small voice filling us with peace, hope, and unconditional love.

Father, stay with us, when dark clouds of fear and anguish engulf us and we are lost and hurting. Draw us into your loving arms and surround us with your comfort and understanding. And when we are feeling at our lowest, unworthy and unlovable, may we feel the warmth and promise of your ever-present love.

AMEN

Take My Life and Let it Be

Take my life, and let it be
Consecrated, Lord, to thee;
Take my moments and my days,
Let them flow in ceaseless praise.

(Frances Ridley Havergal: 1836–79)

*F*rances (Fanny) Havergal was one of that staunch army of Victorian spinster ladies who rose above the limitations of their circumstances to contribute so much to the Christian understanding of others for generations to come. Her home was Astley in rural Worcestershire where her father was rector of the parish church. From the start, her health was frail and her physical energy levels sometimes low – but her mind was constantly active. While she was still a small girl she was already quoting both the Old and New Testaments, and spoke Hebrew and Greek as well as several modern languages – and she was an excellent pianist.

Perhaps she inherited her poor health from her mother, who passed away when Fanny was only eleven years old. Knowing how sensitive her daughter was, her mother gave her some good advice in their last hours together: "Pray God to prepare *you* for all he is preparing *for* you."

After nearly a decade of severe illness which started when she was eighteen, Fanny emerged having decided exactly what God was preparing for her. He'd given her a talent for music and writing – great qualities for a hymn writer – and so she put pen to paper to create unforgettable and poignant hymns such as "Like a River Glorious", "I Am Trusting Thee, Lord Jesus" and "Who is on the Lord's Side?"

However, it is this hymn, "Take My Life and Let it Be", which resounds more than any other with Fanny's heartfelt wish to dedicate her whole life to God's service. Her long struggle with ill health made her acutely aware of her limitations – both physical and practical – and yet she still lists so many ways in which she has something to contribute.

How encouraging these words are to those of us who also struggle to work out how we can be of value to others. Some of us are hampered by ill health or disability. Others find that the demands of either family or working life leave little opportunity for much else. Perhaps we lack confidence in our own abilities and feel that whatever we might give would pale into insignificance against the contributions of others. But God, who made and loves us, knows exactly what we are capable of achieving. He recognizes our insecurities and practical limitations, and he knows that sometimes it's the smallest of gifts which are not only the most sincerely and generously given, but which can also have the greatest impact.

If you're worried that you already have so many calls on your time and energy that you simply don't have the chance to give more of yourself, then remember you're a Christian all day every day, not just on Sundays or whenever else you think about it. "They'll know we are Christians by our love" is a phrase we often hear, and we are surrounded by countless examples of how true that statement is. Anyone who holds in their mind their Christian commitment to care for others will find plenty of opportunities to show that understanding and concern. We need Christians in every walk of life. That doesn't mean Bible-bashing or making others feel uncomfortable in any way; it simply means that we are channels of God's love at all times, and his love will speak for itself. What better endorsement of Christian life can there be than that we show constant care for others, as Christ asked that we should.

Fanny Havergal's life was limited by poor health, and yet her gift of love in hymn writing has inspired generations ever since. Forget about what you *can't* do and think about the unique ways in which you may be able to enrich the lives of others using the talents that God has already prepared for you.

> *Take my love; my Lord, I pour*
> *At thy feet its treasure-store;*
> *Take myself, and I will be,*
> *Ever, only, all for thee.*

> AMEN

Eternal Father

Eternal Father, strong to save,
Whose arm doth bind the restless wave,
Who bidd'st the mighty ocean deep
Its own appointed limits keep;
O hear us when we cry to thee
For those in peril on the sea.

(William Whiting: 1825–78)

I come from a naval family. My childhood was spent travelling from one port to another, wherever my father was based. With each new posting came the upheaval of a house move and starting at a new school. This was never easy, but wherever we went, I would find other pupils who were living exactly the same lifestyle, and it turned out that classmates from my infant school in Plymouth were also at my junior school in Malta, and in sixth form with me in Gosport on the edge of Portsmouth Harbour.

It's not surprising that "Eternal Father" was the unofficial school hymn everywhere we went, because it was so relevant to us. Many of my friends' fathers were part of the Polaris submarine team, which meant that they would disappear off the face of the earth for months at a time, mostly unable to keep in touch with the family back home. Imagine how their sons and daughters felt as they sang these words! Just a look at the waters of the Solent outside the school hall window would make the power and fury of the elements frighteningly obvious, so this prayer calling for God's protection for all at sea was deeply touching.

Surprisingly, though, William Whiting who penned these words was a bit of a landlubber! For thirty-six years he was master of the Quiristers of Winchester College, a group of boys whose official duty was to sing in the chapel but who were in fact little more than unpaid servants to the young gentlemen attending the college. It's said that William wrote this text for one of the young quiristers who was about to embark on the long sea voyage across to America.

In 1963, "Eternal Father" was played as President John F. Kennedy's body was carried up the steps of the US Capitol to lie in state after his assassination. Kennedy had been a naval officer himself, and had a strong sense of belonging to the sea. He once wrote:

*We are tied to the ocean. And when we go back
to the sea, whether it is to sail or to watch, we are
going back from whence we came.*

On his desk in the Oval Office, he kept a plaque which
had been given to him by an admiral who would make
a similar gift to any new submarine captain. The words
came from Breton fishermen for whom this was a heartfelt
prayer:

Lord, thy sea is so great and my boat is so small.

We don't need to be sailors on the high seas to recognize
that feeling of being thrown around by the storms of life –
sailing peacefully one minute then being knocked off our
feet by insecurity, arguments, disappointment, betrayal,
failure, and exhaustion. It's at times like those, when fear
engulfs us, that we can feel utterly alone and abandoned.

Do you remember, though, how afraid the disciples
were when their boat hit a storm on the Sea of Galilee –
and all the time, Jesus was fast asleep on a cushion?

"Don't you care if we drown?" they yelled when
he finally awoke, then watched in amazement as Christ
ordered the wind and waves to be still.

"Why are you so afraid?" he asked. "Do you still have
no faith?" (Mark 4:37–40).

In fairness, the disciples were only just getting
to know Jesus so could be forgiven for not yet having
complete trust in his promises. We, however, know how

the glorious story of Christ continues, so we have every reason to trust that he is always with us, and that we *can* rely on his loving care and protection.

> *Father, when we feel small and helpless, surrounded by a frightening world, we pray for your loving protection to calm our fears, just as you stilled the waters of Galilee. There are so many ways in which you reassure us of your presence. Help us to trust in you always.*
>
> AMEN

Be Thou My Vision

Be thou my vision, O Lord of my heart,
Be all else but naught to me, save that thou art,
Be thou my best thought in the day and the night,
Both waking and sleeping, thy presence my light.

(Old Irish poem, Tr. Mary Byrne: 1880–1931
and Eleanor Hull: 1860–1935)

*O*ver all my years of presenting *Songs of Praise*, I can't tell you how often this hymn was the first choice of the people I interviewed. Most of us, as we look back over our lives, wish we'd had better insight, more warning, less confusion, greater abilities during times when we found ourselves facing challenges and difficulties. How wonderful it would have been if we'd had someone on our side, guiding us through, helping us to overcome obstacles along the way! Even better, we long for God's guidance to unveil our vision and to point us in the direction we should choose.

The true origin of these words is lost in the mists of time, but there's a common belief in Ireland that they date back to a sixth-century poem that is said to have been written by Saint Dallan Forgaill. His real name was Eochaid, and he was a descendant of High King Colla Uais. However, he was always known by his nickname Dallan, which meant "little blind one", after he lost his sight – reputedly as a result of studying too much.

In spite of his poor eyesight, Dallan's knowledge of Latin Scripture and his skill as a poet led to him being asked to become Chief Ollam of Ireland, the leading bard of literature and history across the land. By the time he was in his late sixties, he was based on the island of Inniskeel in County Donegal where, in 598, pirates attacked the monastery. The legend goes that Dallan was beheaded, but that God reattached his head to his body after he was martyred. Five centuries later he was acclaimed a saint and his words have been providing inspiration ever since.

In his poem, he lists all that he felt he needed then – and all that we need now. He asks for God to be the focus of his thoughts, whether he's asleep or awake. He hopes for wisdom and honesty, and for holy protection in what he describes as a battle in life between good and evil. He calls out to God as his father, imagining that they might dwell together, father and devoted son. He shuns the emptiness of riches and false praise, because he recognizes God as the only inheritance he'll ever need. And he asks that the

Sovereign of heaven should be in his heart, guiding him towards the bright Sun once the battle of life is over.

Most moving of all, Dallan prays for vision – something that must have had very special meaning to a man who was blind. Yet it's not physical vision he yearns for, but spiritual vision to make the right choices and take the best path throughout his life. That's the kind of vision we all need, to make judgments not based on worldly surroundings and values, but according to the guidance and will of God.

This hymn is a heartfelt prayer from beginning to end, but let's concentrate our thoughts in prayer on what is asked of God in the second verse, the one I always find most moving:

> *Be thou my wisdom, be thou my true word,*
> *Be thou ever with me, and I with thee, Lord.*
> *Be thou my great Father, and I thy true son,*
> *Be thou in me dwelling, and I with thee one.*

AMEN

Tell Me the Old, Old Story

Tell me the old, old story of unseen things above,
Of Jesus and his glory, of Jesus and his love.
Tell me the story simply, as to a little child,
For I am weak and weary, and helpless and
defiled.

Tell me the old, old story, tell me the old, old
story,
Tell me the old, old story, of Jesus and his love.

(Arabella Catherine Hankey: 1834–1911)

*P*rime Minister William Gladstone was giving a lecture on the subject of Science, Industry, and Art. During his speech, he said that he didn't think any of these could relieve the sorrow of human life or combat the evils that defiled the world. He said:

If I am asked what is the remedy for such things,
I must point to something which, in a well-known
hymn, is called The Old, Old Story, told of in

an old, old book, and taught with an old, old teaching, which is the greatest gift ever given to mankind.

It was a longing to hear that old, old story while laid low by illness that Kate Hankey was moved to write this children's hymn which has been translated into more languages than any other. She was the well-educated daughter of a prosperous banker and first started teaching at a Sunday School in Croydon in South London. Then she went on to start a Bible class for shop assistants in large West End department stores. She was only thirty when a sudden serious illness left her so weak and weary that she felt like a child, needing "simple thoughts in simple words", which is all any of us can cope with when we're unwell.

In her loneliness, Kate longed for someone to come and remind her of that old, old story – but in the end she did it herself by writing a two-part poem with fifty verses, which included the words of this hymn.

Many of us learn the basic truths of our Christian faith as children, when we are told Bible stories, learn to say our prayers, and sing hymns with words that stay in our minds forever. As we grow older and are more able to think for ourselves, we may study and question more, and through experience, establish our own relationship with and understanding of God.

William Gladstone and Kate Hankey learned about the gospel of Christ in a very different way to that in which children learn it today. There is infinite choice within our churches now, with styles of worship that range from rock bands to cathedral choirs, from traditional hymns to modern choruses, and from smells and bells to services which flow freely and without a set form as the Spirit moves among the congregation. Our style of worship is likely to reflect our culture and traditions as well as our individual choice of atmosphere and content. What becomes clear is that there is no right way to praise the Lord, as I feel sure our worship is always welcomed as long as it is sincere and honest.

The main thing is that we never forget the old, old story. It may be more than 2,000 years since Jesus lived on earth and rose to heaven, but the truth and the triumph of his coming, his death, and his resurrection can never change. We might now read our Bible on a Kindle, or receive daily devotional prayers through the internet. Our children may grow up learning at school as much about the other great faiths of the world as they do about Christianity – but the old, old story of Christ coming to earth to live among us, and die for us, is the eternal truth, longed for by Kate Hankey and recognized by William Gladstone as the greatest gift and blessing of all.

Lord, our world is changing fast. We have learned so much, and yet know so little. We can get lost among all the information that comes our way so that we lose

sight of the most important thing we need to know –
that Christ lived with us on earth, died for our sins,
and reigns on high forever. Hallelujah!

AMEN

O for a Thousand Tongues to Sing

O for a thousand tongues to sing
My dear Redeemer's praise,
The glories of my God and King,
The triumphs of his grace!

(Charles Wesley: 1707–88)

*H*ave you ever sung this glorious hymn in a wonderful cathedral where the fellowship of voices and musicians resound around the ancient walls? On *Songs of Praise*, that has happened to me many times, and I find myself thinking how much Charles Wesley would have loved to be part of that experience.

He wrote thousands of hymns and travelled many more thousands of miles taking the good news of the gospel the length and breadth of Britain. On his travels, he must have met so many people and drawn from their wide range of experiences and customs in worship as he wrote one hymn of praise after another. When he wrote this great hymn about a thousand voices raised together in praise, I wonder if he imagined those voices raised in total harmony and fellowship.

But in reality, Charles knew as well as we do today that, although we all describe ourselves as Christians, our understanding of what that means can vary greatly. I remember being very moved when a remarkable young Christian man from the Sudan told me of the awful torture and persecution he had suffered for his faith. His story had a wonderful new beginning when he, his wife, and baby son were rescued by British Christians and brought to England to start a new life. His expression became perplexed as he explained what he thought of the Christians he met here. Where he'd come from, he told me, just to meet another person who believed in Christ as their saviour was more than enough! "Here," he said, "people sit in their different churches niggling about the detail that divides them rather than the truth that unites."

He does have a point. We are very comfortable in our faith here. No one challenges our right to be Christians. No one is forcing other beliefs upon us. We have complete freedom to worship as we choose. And he's right that theological and liturgical detail can vary significantly from one denomination to another, to the degree that we can sometimes come across as very judgmental about what is correct and acceptable in the eyes of God. But who are we to say what God would consider acceptable? We can look back down the years to see how the accepted understanding of the teachings of the Bible has changed from generation to generation. God doesn't change – but we have regularly rewritten the rules about what is correct belief and behaviour according to the thinking of the day.

We should never stop trying to fathom the mystery and magnificence of God, nor stop questioning how best we can serve him – and I think we need to do that not *only* with the help and direction of our fellow Christians and teachers, but ultimately also in the personal relationship we develop with God. We were each created to be different and unique, so surely the bond we share with our Creator is unique and personal too. Through the teachings of the Bible and our church, and through our own experience of his faithful presence in our lives, we spend the length of our lifetime working out for ourselves what we truly believe.

And if, as that young Sudanese man suggested, Christians are sometimes divided by our differences rather than united by the faith we share, then perhaps that's when we should draw on all we know from the Gospels about the nature of Christ, and consider what his reaction would be to the different ways in which his life and teaching are interpreted.

I think he would stand with his arms open wide to welcome all, accepting, understanding, loving, and forgiving.

O for a Thousand Tongues to Sing

You know me, Lord. You have held me in the palm of your hand. I pray that I may also learn to know you, and to reflect your love and tolerance in my relationships, my understanding, and my faith. Open my head and mind to your truth so that I may sing with others in perfect harmony.

AMEN

Glad That I Live Am I

Glad that I live am I, that the sky is blue;
Glad for the country lanes and the fall of dew.

After the sun, the rain; after the rain, the sun;
This is the way of life till the work be done.

(Lizette Woodworth Rees: 1856–1935)

I reckon I was without my two front teeth and just starting in infant school when I first heard this hymn. I was growing up in Plymouth, surrounded by West Country landscape rooted in deep red soil, with the wilds of Dartmoor just a short drive away. On Sunday afternoons, our family tradition was to head off for a walk where my challenge was to collect treasures from the countryside that I could take into school the next day for the show and tell table. It was a wonderful chance to see for myself the cycle of the seasons, both in the way the colours and look of the landscape changed, and in the wealth of small detail that a curious five-year-old could find fascinating. I can still feel my sense of triumph on a Monday morning as I carried in a bag full of flowering willows, fat acorns, brightly coloured lichen, or the remains of a bird's nest. And I remember, too, the loving security of being in a happy family group, with parents who helped my brother and me discover the wonders of nature by pointing out what we might miss, and listened patiently to our excited chatter as we made exciting discoveries of our own.

Those country walks instilled in me the habit of always noticing what's happening in the world outside the four walls of home, even if, later in life, that home was far from the countryside. I have fond memories from when my own children were small of how long it would take us to walk down the lane towards their school, because it was lined with hedgerow, shrubs, and grasses which changed daily along with the seasons. In springtime we would check every day to see how quickly the bright green leaves were growing on the bare winter boughs. We'd watch buds fatten and burst into colour – then look for the hawthorn "May" blossom to tell us when we could shed our woollies at the end of winter! The bluebells, the cow parsley, the crawling insects and buzzing bees, the berries which brightened in colour as autumn approached – the children and I noticed every change and relished them all.

These are my "Glad That I Live Am I" moments, golden times in ordinary days when it's suddenly abundantly clear that life is full of small blessings. Do you know that feeling? Whatever prompts it – perhaps the miracle of creation around us, maybe the warmth of family love or friendship, or even a feeling of personal achievement or fulfilment that simply makes us feel good – these are heart-warming moments of what's positive and beautiful in our world. They fill us not just with wonder, but also with a sense of reassurance and security that, however mankind tries to interfere with the ageless cycle of nature, God is in his creation, constant, unchanging, and faithful. How can you look at a sunlit sky or a stormy sea and not see God's power? How can you marvel at the pattern and mechanics of a flower opening or a butterfly's wing in flight without acknowledging the brilliant intricacy and inspiration behind it – a genius which is way beyond human capability even to imagine, let alone create?

For me, those "Glad That I Live Am I" moments are the pinnacle of human experience because, through them, we glimpse God around us, beside us, and with us. No wonder we're glad!

Thank you, Lord, for the splendour of the world around us, and for the beauty and wonder in every tiny detail. May we never take your gifts for granted, but recognize our responsibility to nurture and care for the bounty of life that surround us in so many forms. And may we always value and cherish the blessings of our own lives, for which we give you humble thanks.

AMEN

The Servant Song

Brother, sister, let me serve you,
Let me be as Christ to you;
Pray that I may have the grace to
Let you be my servant too.

I will hold the Christ-light for you
In the night-time of your fear;
I will hold my hand out to you,
Speak the peace you long to hear.

(Richard Gillard: b. 1953)

hen Richard Gillard wrote both the words and music of this song in the seventies, he picked up on a growing feeling among young people that a lot needed to change. This was reflected particularly in the music of the time, both secular and Christian. Challenging songs emerged in which basic truths and personal honesty were expressed not only in unforgettable words, but also in a simple folk style of music which came very naturally to home-taught guitarists like Richard who hoped that his own "down-to-earth groundedness" would shine through "The Servant Song".

This song is typical of that time in that it poignantly portrays how uncaring people had become, a situation which many of us feel has grown worse ever since. Whatever happened to neighbour helping neighbour? Is it just that our working and family lives have become so busy and complex that we have little time or care for much beyond what's already demanded of us? We might be vaguely aware that an elderly lady whom we rarely see lives a few doors down – but would we be interested enough to find out for ourselves that she has little company, frugal finances, and deteriorating health so that every day of her life is filled with gaping loneliness and despair?

There are so many people who live on the fringes of our communities, unreachable in many ways because of their lack of confidence, physical ability, mental health, finances, or company. One day, we could be just like that. *There but for the grace of God...*

At the heart of our Christian faith is a commitment to treat others as we would wish to be treated ourselves – to *be as Christ*, in that he *did not come to be served, but to serve*. It's not enough to say we're too exhausted or too busy to find time to put ourselves out for others. Christ's whole life was the perfect example of humbling himself to serve those in need. He noticed their pain and struggle, and he put his comforting arm around them in empathy and compassion. He charges us to do the same, telling us in Matthew's Gospel that whatever we've done "for one of the least of these brothers and sisters of mine, you did for me" (Matthew 25:40).

Infinite love resounds throughout the verses of this song, with their description of the fellowship, company, and practical care that should be a way of life for all Christians. Immediately, I find myself thinking of wonderful, generous Christian friends whose lives are already devoted to the needs of others, as they quietly get on with small acts of kindness – such as being in the kitchen washing up when everyone else is socializing; regularly taking a meal into a lonely, infirm neighbour; shopping for a disabled friend; looking after lively grandchildren to allow their mother a chance to work; standing outside the supermarket in the cold rattling a collecting tin for a good cause…

Often, such selfless people dismiss their constant generosity as unimportant, brushing aside any recognition or thanks. But this hymn points out that just as we are called in grace to *give*, so we are also called to *receive*. It's easy to get carried away with a sense of our own generosity – but we must take care that those we help aren't left feeling that they are simply the object of our pity and charity. To be able to thank a kind benefactor from the heart allows them dignity and purpose. Everyone deserves that.

The Servant Song

We are pilgrims on a journey,
And companions on the road;
We are here to help each other
Walk the mile and bear the load.

AMEN

O Perfect Love

O perfect Love, all human thought transcending,
Lowly we kneel in prayer before thy throne,
That theirs may be the love that knows no ending
Whom thou for evermore dost join in one.

(Dorothy Gurney: 1858–1932)

*M*any familiar hymns that are sung at weddings speak of love – both godly and earthly – but, oddly enough, this is one of just a few hymns I can think of which is specifically to be sung during the marriage service – and it was written way back in 1883! Those were the days when families would gather around the piano for a good old sing-song, and one Sunday evening Dorothy Gurney's family were thoroughly enjoying working their way through the hymn book. When one particular melody was played, everyone commented on how delightful it was, including Dorothy's sister who issued a challenge.

"What's the use of a sister who composes poetry if she can't write new words to a favourite tune? I would like to use this tune at my wedding!"

Never one to resist a challenge, Dorothy disappeared into another room with a copy of the music and asked that nobody disturb her. Fifteen minutes later, she returned with these words, saying that they needed no effort at all as she felt God had helped her to write the song.

Three years later when the hymn found its way into the *Hymns, Ancient and Modern* hymn book, it became very popular, especially at fashionable weddings, including those of royalty. More importantly, when Dorothy's sister walked down the aisle, she, too, found blessing in both the words and the melody.

In these verses, God is described in two ways – first perfect *love* and then perfect *life*. When we think about it, these descriptions reflect two great ideals which we would hope to find in every Christian marriage. The reason why a bride and groom are choosing to marry and share the rest of their lives together is love. Love is at the heart of everything – not just the love between them, but also the love they share in God, and the love they are blessed with by God. That love sets high standards of fidelity and behaviour expressed as compassionate care for each other and for all others they meet together throughout their lives. A perfect life is their aim, and because of God's perfect love poured on them during the vows and blessings of their wedding ceremony, they pray that they can establish the will and commitment to live well, and to find peace and joy in each other.

That's the ideal, but we all know that our wedding day is not just a happy ending, but also the start of a journey together which will inevitably have a lot of ups and downs along the way. Couples may be married, but they are still two individual people with their own points of view and sets of experiences which shape their opinions and priorities. Lucky the couple who never have a cross word between them, because most of us do, especially when children come along, finances become tight, family and friends fall out, or illness strikes. Then, more than ever, love is all-important. It's probably quite healthy to have different views and even a few angry words once in a while, providing the bottom line is that you love each other unconditionally. When the chips are down, you stand together as the married partners you are.

So my prayer today is for all of us who are married, plan to marry, or perhaps miss being married because, for whatever reason, our partner is no longer with us.

Lord, thank you for the gift of marriage, which allows us to find joy and companionship in being husband and wife. We ask for your blessing as we face whatever life brings our way. May we stand together to celebrate the joyful, proud, and heart-warming moments, and cling together when times are sad or uncertain. Fill our hearts with loving commitment not just for each other, but also for you.

AMEN

Now Thank We All Our God

Now thank we all our God
With heart and hands and voices,
Who wondrous things hath done,
In whom his world rejoices;
Who, from our mother's arms,
Hath blessed us on our way
With countless gifts of love,
And still is ours today.

(Martin Rinkart: 1586–1649)

*I*n many ways, it's incredible that the author of this great hymn of gratitude and praise, Martin Rinkart, could find any reason at all to give thanks to God! He was a pastor in Saxony during the Thirty Years' War, in the walled city of Eilenberg. The city became such an overcrowded refuge for political and military fugitives that it eventually suffered tragically from famine and disease. The worst time was in 1637 when 8,000 people died from plague, including Martin's own wife. By then, he was the only minister left in the town, so he was responsible for conducting burial services for nearly 5,000 people, sometimes as many as fifty a day.

To make matters worse, Eilenberg was overrun or besieged three times, once by the Austrian army and twice by the Swedes. The Swedish general demanded a huge payment of 30,000 thalers from the townspeople. Exhausted by grief, hunger, and despair, they had no chance of raising such a sum, and Martin's plea for compassion fell on deaf ears. So he gathered his people around him saying that, because they could find no mercy with man, they should take refuge in God. As they fell to their knees in heartfelt prayer, the Swedish commander was so moved that he decided to reduce the levy to just 1,350 thalers.

One story goes that Martin wrote these wonderful words of thanks and praise immediately after hearing that decision – but would *you*, after long years of violence, fear, and terrible hardship, be able to write verses that ring with such depths of faith and gratitude? Wouldn't the loss of those you love and the cruelty of your aggressors shake your belief? How could a loving God allow an innocent, helpless community to face such testing times of pain and despair? Had Martin become so immune to heartache over the years that he was desensitized to pain, both in himself and in others?

Quite the opposite! The only thing that kept Martin going during the worst times was his certain knowledge that God was with them. That gave him the strength to support, comfort, and encourage his congregation in their fear and despair, inspiring in them the belief that, in spite of the evil and cruelty they saw around them, God's love was always with them, however much they were tempted to doubt it. God was with them, with those they loved and those they lost – and because of that unshakeable belief, their enemies could only break their bodies, never their spirit.

In our own lives, many of us recognize the truth of this from our most painful times of fear and despair. Isn't it in those darkest moments, when we feel helpless and lost, that we sense God's love most keenly? I wonder how often Martin kept in his heart the words of Paul, who endured years of being beaten, stoned, and imprisoned for his faith, but whose belief in the natural goodness of people and of the unchanging nature of God's love grew stronger day by day? In our most challenging times, when we need to feel the reassurance of God's love in order to keep going, let's remember this prayer based on what Paul said in Romans 5:3–5 (ESV UK).

We rejoice in our sufferings, knowing that suffering produces endurance, and endurance produces character, and character produces hope, and hope does not put us to shame, because God's love has been poured into our hearts through the Holy Spirit who has been given to us.

AMEN

I Heard the Voice of Jesus Say

I heard the voice of Jesus say,
"Come unto me and rest;
Lay down, thou weary one, lay down
Thy head upon my breast."
I came to Jesus as I was,
Weary, and worn, and sad;
I found in him a resting-place,
And he has made me glad.

(Horatius Bonar: 1808–89)

*O*h, don't we all know that feeling of being weary, worn, and sad?! Not just physically exhausted, but the kind of weariness that plummets different depths, where, both emotionally and spiritually, we are running on empty.

Horatius Bonar certainly knew that feeling, because this Victorian Church of Scotland minister and his wife Jane endured times of great sadness during their forty years together. Can you imagine how they must have felt when, one by one, five of their beloved children died while they were still very young? The grief and despair must have been overwhelming at times, to the degree that many people would have found it difficult to believe a loving God would allow such suffering, both for their innocent children and for them as parents. Dr Bonar's response, though, was complete acceptance and trust that God was with them in their loss. He wrote, "Spare not the stroke. Do with me as thou wilt. Let there be naught unfinished, broken or marred. Complete thy purpose that we may become thy perfect image."

Those were brave and faithful words from a man who clearly loved children: many of the 600 hymns he wrote had children in mind. He particularly noticed how bored they would get during the rather monotonous chanting of psalms in their services – so he listened to the tunes children would sing when they weren't in church, and wrote new Christian words which they could sing along to those melodies. In fact, his faith has been described as "childlike", in spite of his powerful intellect and his tall, imposing frame. His parishioners spoke of what a gentle, sympathetic man he was – a good listener who could empathize with their fears and concerns, and reassure them of God's constant love and faithfulness.

There can be many things in our everyday lives that make us feel overwhelmed by grinding weariness. Relationships and family life can be difficult. Work and routine may feel oppressive. Grief, loneliness, ill health, money troubles – all these can lay us low, sapping our energy, draining our resources, and challenging our faith in ourselves and the world around us. At such times, it can feel as if we're falling down a dark tunnel, with no hope of relief and no light on the horizon to draw us in the right direction.

This hymn describes that feeling exactly, but then responds with the recognition that it's not just physical comfort we need, but also a healing of the spirit. Our souls long for the voice of Christ who made us and knows us, and who calls us to take shelter in his loving arms. There we can find rest and living water, light, hope, and infinite comfort.

So our prayer today is the second verse of this wonderfully reassuring hymn. Take comfort in it, because these words were written by a man who knew despair and sadness, just as we do.

I heard the voice of Jesus say,
"Behold, I freely give
The living water; thirsty one,
Stoop down and drink, and live."
I came to Jesus, and I drank
Of that life-giving stream;
My thirst was quenched, my soul revived,
And now I live in him.

AMEN

Abide with Me

Abide with me: fast falls the eventide;
The darkness deepens; Lord, with me abide,
When other helpers fail, and comforts flee,
Help of the helpless, O abide with me.

(Henry Francis Lyte: 1793–1847)

I think of hymns as "prayers in your pocket". When we're going through times of great emotion, pain, or fear, with our minds too muddled to form words of our own prayer or to remember exactly the Bible quotation we need, lines of hymn text often push themselves to the front of our thoughts, expressing in a beautifully poetic way exactly what we want to say.

Never is that more true than with the verses of this dearly loved hymn, "Abide with Me". On countless occasions on *Songs of Praise* when I have been talking to people who are confronted with their mortality as their death approaches, or who have had to mark the death of someone else in difficult circumstances, they have spoken movingly of how singing or even just speaking out loud the words of this hymn brought a real sense of God's presence and comfort.

I remember one D-Day veteran telling me how these words were ringing around his head in silent prayer as he waited to disembark the landing crafts on the Normandy beaches, wondering whether he would be dead before he reached the shore. A young mother living in Moss Side during the riots in 1981 explained how she comforted her two terrified young children with this hymn as fires broke out and cars were smashed outside their home. And three eighty-year-olds who'd survived being Japanese prisoners of war in the Second World War cried openly as they remembered how they'd sung this hymn during the makeshift Christian services they held to mark the loss of yet another comrade who had been cruelly beaten to death by their captors, each mourner knowing that he could be next.

These words have the power to touch raw nerves, perhaps because Henry Lyte knew as he wrote them that his own death was imminent. He was the minister at All Souls Church in the small fishing town of Lower Brixham in Devon, and he had long suffered a weakness in his lungs which had wearied him and worn him down. For some years, his family persuaded him to spend the winter months in Europe where the warmer weather helped his condition, but by the autumn of 1847, as once again they planned his winter voyage, he described himself as "just able to crawl". With the almost unbearable prospect of the long journey looming the following day, he insisted on taking the evening service before walking out at sunset along the shore, knowing that he was unlikely ever to see it again. Later that night he wrote the words of "Abide with Me" and handed the manuscript to his daughter before he left for France the next morning. A little more than two months later, in the town of Nice, Henry died from consumption.

From the start, "Abide with Me" became known as "The Evening Hymn", perhaps because when Henry wrote it that night he knew he was saying goodbye to the place and people he loved. More likely, though, he was acutely aware as he watched the sun set over Brixham that he was in the evening of his own life, and that a difficult time lay ahead. Christians have nothing to fear beyond death – but the actual process of dying, with the pain, long-term suffering, and indignity it might involve terrified Henry, just as it does us all. In these words, with searing honesty, he expresses that fear in a way which goes right to the heart of what we all feel. He balances that acknowledgment of fear with the certain belief that "through cloud and sunshine", the God "who changest not" will be our "guide and stay".

Abide with Me

I fear no foe, with thee at hand to bless;
Ills have no weight, and tears no bitterness.
Where is death's sting? Where, grave, thy victory?
I triumph still, if thou abide with me.

AMEN

Father, Hear the Prayer We Offer

Father, hear the prayer we offer:
Not for ease that prayer shall be,
But for strength that we may ever
Live our lives courageously.

Be our strength in hours of weakness,
In our wanderings be our guide;
Through endeavour, failure, danger,
Father, be thou at our side.

(Love Maria Willis: 1824–1908)

*C*an you imagine living without prayer? Does prayer feel to you, as it does to me, as natural as sleeping, eating, or thinking? In fact, thinking often becomes a prayer in my mind. I feel as if my life is one long conversation with God – and it's never a one-sided chat because I always sense the reassurance of his presence, listening to me, caring for me, and knowing more about me than I could ever know myself.

So when people say they don't believe in God and therefore have never felt the need to pray, I wonder whether they're being completely honest with themselves, because it seems to me that just as our bodies long to sleep or eat, so our souls long to pray.

I particularly remember one old soldier I met through *Songs of Praise* who described the agony of waiting in the landing crafts just off the Normandy coast on D-Day. Like all the young soldiers on board, he was terrified, although nobody dared voice their fear in front of their comrades. He faced the possibility that he was about to die. At the very least, he expected to be injured, perhaps left for dead on enemy soil. He described how he was shaking uncontrollably, petrified by how unready and hopeless he felt. And, in fact, he had no hope. He wasn't a Christian. He didn't believe there was a God. If he were to die that day, he didn't expect there to be anything beyond death for him. So why was it, then, in that moment of dire need and humanity, he found himself praying? His plea to the God he didn't believe in was raw and urgent and desperate: "Let me live! Keep me safe! Keep us all safe! If you're there, if you can hear me, God, bless us please!"

The young man lived that day and through the fearful days that followed – and when eventually he came home, he knew he was changed not just by the horror of war, but also by the wonder of discovering that prayers are heard and answered by the God he went on to worship for the rest of his life.

But we don't need to be soldiers facing death to know we need strength and courage to face the day ahead. For many people, everyday life is a constant challenge. Illness, money problems, family friction, lack of purpose or worth – they can all grind us down so that we feel lost, friendless, without hope or comfort. Love Maria Willis, who wrote this hymn, was kept busy as a doctor's wife in Rochester, New York. She was a mum who knew what it was like to have a husband to support, demanding children to care for, meals to cook, and a house to run. She went through the same exhaustion and frustration we all do – and she prayed about it. In this hymn, she acknowledges the difficulties she faces, and she talks about how she sometimes feels weak, lost, or a failure – but she's not expecting God to take those difficulties away. She asks that the prayer she offers should not be "for ease", because she knows it's through challenge that we discover our own strengths and abilities, and the unique set of skills, qualities, and limitations that God gave each one of us. We have to *learn* what he *knows* – that we have already been blessed with everything we need to cope.

Father, hear my prayer. Even though at times I doubt you and feel overwhelmed with worry, dread, and weariness, please stay with me. Give me courage to face my fears, strength for the road ahead, and confidence that, with your presence and blessing, I will be able to cope.

AMEN

A Mighty Fortress is Our God

A mighty fortress is our God, a bulwark never
*   failing;*
Our helper he, amid the flood of mortal ills
*   prevailing:*
For still our ancient foe doth seek to work us woe;
His craft and power are great, and, armed with
*   cruel hate,*
On earth is not his equal.

(Martin Luther: 1483–1546)

When Martin Luther was born in Mansfeld, Germany, in the middle of the fifteenth century, his father, who had risen from peasant stock to own a copper mine, had high hopes of his son going into the civil service as a lawyer. Martin was nearly qualified when one afternoon in 1505 he was almost struck by lightning in a sudden thunderstorm. He was so frightened he threw up a promise that if he was spared, he would become a monk. He lived to tell the tale, but immediately regretted his words because he had to drop out of law school to enter the monastery.

However, Martin's monastic studies soon had him questioning the accepted teaching of the Catholic Church, especially the suggestion that the forgiveness of sins and God's salvation could be bartered for and purchased through financial *indulgences*. As he studied the Psalms and Paul's letters in the Latin Bible, he came to the belief that God's favour is a gift to be accepted rather than a prize to be bought or won. On Hallowe'en of 1517, he nailed to the church door in Wittenberg a sheet listing his *Ninety-five Theses*, which eventually formed the basic ethos of the new Protestant movement that swept across the world.

Luther experienced for himself a personal relationship with God, and he encouraged that experience in others by reforming the routine of church services. He shepherded in the idea of preaching for congregations who mostly could not read, especially from Bibles written only in Latin. He was the first person to translate the Bible into a local commonly spoken language, and it's his inspiration we have to thank for our own English translation.

But Martin also recognized the value of another wonderful way of learning about the Scriptures and expressing them in fellowship with other worshippers within our churches. He introduced congregational singing, and wrote his own hymn book of nearly forty hymns. It's said that at the beginning of one his sermons, Martin Luther held up a Bible and declared, "This is the gospel." Then he raised his other hand, in which he held a hymn book, and said, "And this is how we remember it."

Psalm 46 was his inspiration as he wrote "A Mighty Fortress is Our God", but almost immediately this hymn became a rallying call for the Reformation. It was sung in the streets, by poor Protestant emigrants on their way to exile, and by martyrs at their deaths. It is confident and defiant, just like Luther himself. Martin was a humble Augustinian monk in a corner of Germany, and yet his courage in speaking out for what he believed quite literally changed Christianity around the world in a way he could never have imagined at the outset.

Often we feel we're too insignificant and powerless for our opinions and beliefs to be heard. Who would want to listen to us? What difference could we possibly make? But if what we believe is true and right, then our message has its own purpose and power. In prayer and faith, Martin spoke out about what he saw to be the true nature of our forgiving, loving God, and his words touched the hearts and souls of millions.

Inspired by that young monk, we may find our courage, too, in the knowledge that God will support and guide us if we are brave and committed enough to stand up for compassion and righteousness.

Father, help us to know your truth, and to be bold enough to speak it loud and clear. Give us courage in the face of ridicule or attack, to think not of ourselves, but of those who need to know of your precious gift to us in your Son, Jesus Christ our Lord. May we never stop singing your praises!

AMEN

Fight the Good Fight

Fight the good fight with all thy might;
Christ is thy strength, and Christ thy right;
Lay hold on life, and it shall be
Thy joy and crown eternally.

(John Samuel Bewley Monsell: 1811–75)

*T*he "fight" John Monsell had in mind is not a call to battle. This is a prayer for steady faithfulness, a quality John showed in abundance throughout his life. He came from good Irish stock, as his father was the Archdeacon of Derry, so perhaps it's no surprise that both he and his brother Charles went into ministry themselves.

Life presented John and his wife Anne with plenty of challenges over the years. In 1855, their eldest son, Thomas, was just eighteen when he died in a shipwreck off Italy on his way to the Crimean War. Six years later, their eldest daughter, Elizabeth, died in Torquay at the age of twenty-eight. Such a double loss to loving parents must have tested John and Anne to the extreme, not just in their relationship with each other, but also in their relationship with God. It would be nothing less than a fight to cope with the tragic impact this had on their family life.

John was certainly one to roll up his sleeves and get stuck into work, though. At all three of his churches – first in County Antrim, then at Egham in Surrey, and finally at St Nicholas Church in nearby Guildford – he undertook major building projects. At St Nicholas, he climbed on to the roof to speak to builders, but he missed his footing and fell to the ground. Because of his injuries, John eventually lost his fight for life.

Generally speaking, the fights we find ourselves facing are mostly domestic. Differences of opinion and even heated arguments can blow up when family members, friends, or colleagues, all with different experiences, personalities, and perspectives, simply can't agree. As each of us is unique, of course there will be times when one person's priority differs completely from the viewpoints of others. We all express our thoughts as the individuals we are, so the person who shouts loudest may overpower the points made by someone who is quieter and less forceful. People who argue may *hear* what the other person is saying, but they rarely *listen* because, for them, the most important thing is that *their* message should be heard above all else.

So, is it possible to have a *good fight*?

As Christians, we're taught to treat others as we would wish to be treated. That means respect and friendship should be the bottom line of all relationships, so any actions or conversations we have should take place within that context. Sometimes tempers do boil over, and although we may not always like what we hear, we may have to agree to differ until the atmosphere is calmer and we can work together to move on.

I've learned over my years of being a mum that little is achieved in a highly charged argument. When my daughter was a teenager and prone to emotional outbursts about how *life* – and, in particular, how *I* – wasn't fair, I'd let her cool down a bit before I knocked on her door with a cup of tea and a bacon butty! It always worked. We'd end up sitting on her bed for as long as we needed, talking things over constructively, with lots of hugs and apologies on both sides.

That little word "sorry" has a lot of power. It may not change the facts of the argument, but it makes for an atmosphere in which discussion is possible. If the worst arguments we have are with someone we love, let's remember as we shout out our opinion that we *do* love them. Let's separate the harsh words from the love we will always feel for them. Remember, God is in us all. Look for him if you really do want the fight to be a *good* one.

Fight the Good Fight

Faint not nor fear, his arms are near;
He changest not and thou art dear;
Only believe, and thou shalt see
That Christ is all in all to thee.

AMEN

Be Still, for the Presence of the Lord

Be still, for the presence of the Lord,
The holy one, is here:
Come bow before him now
With reverence and fear:
In him no sin is found –
We stand on holy ground.
Be still, for the presence of the Lord,
The holy one, is here.

(David J. Evans: b. 1957)

*T*he power of this disarmingly simple song is the depth of its meaning combined with the ease with which it comes to mind whenever we need it. In God, wherever we are is "holy ground", and there are times in all our lives when we find ourselves just wanting to stop still for a moment and allow ourselves to sense God's constant presence and love.

I have one particularly moving memory of the impact of this song. It was 31 August 1997, that Sunday morning when we all woke up to the shocking news of Princess Diana's death. I received an early morning call to say that *Songs of Praise* was planning a live edition of the programme that evening from St Paul's Cathedral. I've never been more proud to be part of the BBC team than on that day. It usually takes three days to light that magnificent building, but our lads did the job in three hours. Our production team worked with the clergy at St Paul's to decide just what the content of the programme should be, and in that respect *Songs of Praise* was fulfilling the role in which it excels. Whenever there's a shared emotion across the country – grief, fear, or celebration – our aim is to gather together people's thoughts and feelings, then weave them into words and music that offer Christian comfort, understanding, and guidance. This is particularly true in a live programme when, as we pray, millions across the country are praying with us.

As we went on air that evening, I felt a real sense of moment as I introduced the programme in front of a packed cathedral in which the congregation were unusually sombre and silent. It was a deeply moving experience for us all as readings and prayers led into choir pieces and congregational hymns. At one point, it seemed we might lose our transmission as news came that the plane carrying Diana's body from Paris had arrived in

England. In the end, our music was allowed to continue over the pictures of the plane landing. The poignancy of the event was self-evident. No further words were needed.

As the programme ended, the congregation drifted out, the choir and clergy went home, and only our BBC team were left clearing equipment away, when we realized that great cathedral was filling up again. Churches all over the country spoke of the same experience – but where do you go when you are shocked into facing the big questions of life, except to church? Before long, more than a thousand people were filling the pews of St Paul's, with no one there to minister to them. Suddenly, a pure, clear voice rang out across the cathedral as what sounded like a young woman had obviously found an open mic and started singing "Be Still for the Presence of the Lord". Its spiritual depth combined with the simplicity of both the melody and the delivery created a prayerful atmosphere in which none of us doubted that "the holy one" was indeed there.

I believe that wherever we are is a holy place, because God never leaves us. It is we who forget him as we bustle about our daily lives. We only have to stop, be still, and clear the clutter of the day from our minds, to approach God in prayer and find he's been there all along. In the face of our inconstancy, he is a constant presence, sharing our joy, comforting our sadness, and guiding us with protection and encouragement.

Be Still, for the Presence of the Lord

O Holy One, stay with me, even when the demands of daily life turn my thoughts from you. And when the day is done, breathe peace into my mind and heart so that I can find you in the stillness of prayer.

AMEN

How Great Thou Art

O Lord my God, when I in awesome wonder
Consider all the works thy hand hath made,
I see the stars, I hear the mighty thunder,
Thy power throughout the universe displayed:

Then sings my soul, my Saviour God, to thee,
How great thou art, how great thou art!
Then sings my soul, my Saviour God, to thee,
How great thou art, how great thou art!

(Carl Boberg: 1859–1940, translated
by Stuart Hine: 1899–1989)

*L*iving among the majestic hills and valleys of Sweden, Carl Boberg was well known not only as a senator in the Swedish parliament for fifteen years, but also as a poet. One day in 1885 when he was walking home from his church near Kronoback, he was caught in a sudden thunderstorm that erupted with violent power around him. Just as quickly, the storm subsided to a peaceful calm as a rainbow arched over Monsteras Bay. Arriving home, the minister opened his window to hear birdsong, and church bells pealing in the still evening air – and he sat down there and then to write the words of this hymn.

Over the years, translations were made into German and Russian, and it was in western Ukraine in 1927 that Salvationist missionaries Stuart Hine and his wife Edith came across the song in Russian. In time, Stuart translated three verses into English, creating the majority of the hymn which is so dear to us today, before the Hines eventually left Eastern Europe at the outbreak of World War Two.

Nearly a decade later when Stuart was visiting a camp in Sussex where refugees from Eastern Europe were being held, he talked to one Russian man who told how he'd not seen his wife since he'd been separated from her at the end of the war. His wife was a Christian, while he was not – but in the intervening years he'd found faith, and he longed to share his belief with her. Sadly, he realized he was unlikely to meet her again in this world, but he believed they would be together in heaven. It was that man's simple trust that inspired Stuart to write the final verse about the joy that will fill our hearts as Christ comes at last to take us home.

"How Great Thou Art", which has been top of the *Songs of Praise* poll of favourite hymns in the UK for all the years I've presented the programme, might never have travelled further if it hadn't reached the hand of George Beverley Shea, the much-loved gospel singer who led the music at the Billy Graham rallies for many years. When he introduced it at the New York Crusade in 1957, it was sung no less than ninety-nine times, setting it on course to become probably the world's favourite hymn.

Why do people love it so? Perhaps because of the vibrant picture it paints of the majesty, power, and splendour of creation, which can erupt into violent storms with a savagery that shakes us one minute, then calms to peaceful beauty the next. It was in both the vast power and the tiny detail that Carl Boberg saw the greatness of God and expressed in poetry the way in which that experience lifted his soul to think not just of those gifts, but also of the greatest gift God has ever given us. There is deep emotion in the third verse as Carl finds it unbelievable that, for his sake and for the sake of us all, God sent his own Son to die, taking upon himself the burden of all our sins on the cross as his blood flowed and his life ebbed away. In these words we find the heart of our faith – our sense of immense gratitude and wonder that the God who wields power over the universe should also feel such intimate and unconditional love for each and every one of us.

And when I think that God, his Son not sparing,
Sent him to die – I scarce can take it in,
That on the cross, my burden gladly bearing,
He bled and died to take away my sin.

God, how great thou art!

AMEN

Blest Be the Tie That Binds

*Blest be the tie that binds our hearts in Christian
    love;*
*The fellowship of kindred minds is like to that
    above.*
*Before our Father's throne we pour our ardent
    prayers;*
*Our fears, our hopes, our aims are one, our
    comforts and our cares.*

(John Fawcett: 1740–1817)

*P*erhaps it was John Fawcett's humble start in life that gave him the compassion and love for others that pours out of every line of this hymn. Who would have thought that a man who became one of the greatest scholars in the land, a published author, and the founder of a school for young preachers, had been orphaned at the age of twelve and sent to work for fourteen hours a day in a sweat shop exploiting child labour? But John knew he wanted more, and at the end of each day he taught himself to read by candlelight, determined to improve his education.

Ordination was both a mission and a step up in life. By the time he was twenty-six, he brought his new bride, Mary, to where he took up his first post at a Baptist church in Wainsgate. The congregation was so poor, his salary was partly paid in potatoes and wool.

Seven years later, John's talent as a preacher was widely recognized, and he was asked to take over as the minister of the influential Carter Lane Church in London. On the day of their departure, Mary and he loaded all their furniture and possessions onto the horse and dray, as their heartbroken congregation stood alongside to say goodbye. John looked around at the young couples he had married, the children he had baptized, the elderly whose sorrows and concerns he'd shared, and the families he'd comforted through sickness and bereavement. These were simple, honest, humble people, few of whom could read or write – and his heart lurched at the thought of abandoning them. In the end, Mary and he agreed that the dray should be unloaded and that they would stay just a little longer. That stay lasted another fifty-four years until his death.

John became well known as a writer, even to King George III who was so impressed by an essay he wrote about "Anger" that he offered John anything a monarch could bestow. The offer was politely refused in John's letter of reply:

I have lived among my own people, enjoying their love. God has blessed my labours among them and I need nothing which even a King could supply.

In today's materialistic society, true compassion and humility like John's are hard to find. Perhaps it's because we don't know our neighbours as we used to? Nowadays, it's not uncommon for an elderly person living on their own to be engulfed in soul-destroying loneliness in a street where every other house is full of people who are so busy with their own lives that they don't consider for one moment any needs beyond their own. Perhaps we're all feeling the pinch in our pockets too much to share what we have with others? Perhaps twenty-four-hour news coverage has numbed us to the plight of our world neighbours whose lives are torn apart by civil war, persecution, drought, poverty, and hunger? When we hear of children abused, families torn apart, or young people running amok in our towns, we instantly demand that someone should be doing something, never thinking for one minute that that someone should be us! It's easy to have opinions about what should be done – much harder to put ourselves on the line.

Yet Christ demands nothing less of us than that we treat others as we wish to be treated ourselves – so let's pray today for the sensitivity to recognize the world of need around us, and for determination to make a positive difference wherever we can:

Christ, you were born on earth into poverty. You often chose the company of those who stood on the edges of society – shunned, diseased, fearful, alone, and confused. Open our eyes to the needs of those around us. Give us the perception, the will, and the ability to follow your commandment that we should love our neighbours as ourselves.

AMEN

To God Be the Glory

To God be the glory, great things he hath done!
So loved he the world that he gave us his Son,
Who yielded his life in atonement for sin,
And opened the life-gate that all may go in.

Praise the Lord! Praise the Lord! Let the earth
            hear his voice!
Praise the Lord! Praise the Lord! Let the people
            rejoice!
O come to the Father, through Jesus the Son;
And give him the glory – great things he hath
            done!

(Fanny Crosby: 1820–1915)

hat's in a name? In hymn writing, probably quite a lot, because some of my favourite writers of hymns have wonderful, resounding names, such as Augustus Toplady and Thomas Obadiah Chisholm! The name I'm thinking of in this instance, though, is Frances – the Christian name of three women who made unforgettable contributions to our hymn books.

The first *Frances* was officially credited by her married name of Frances van Alstyne, but for the 8,000 or more hymn texts she wrote, she was always simply known as Fanny Crosby. In spite of the fact that she was blinded within days of her birth, her mind was racing with ways in which she wanted to thank God for all the countless blessings that surrounded her. Sometimes she wrote three texts a day, all of them full of thanks and praise, and because her hymns became so well known and loved during her lifetime, they were immediately set to music and became favourites across the world.

They even reached a rather frail English lady living in the beautiful village of Astley in rural Worcestershire where her father was rector. Also called *Frances*, she too was affectionately known by her family as *Fanny*. She was sixteen years younger than the American writer she admired so much, and her ongoing ill health claimed her life when she was only in her early forties, unlike Fanny Crosby who was still writing until she died in her nineties! There were times in Fanny Havergal's life when she felt her lack of physical health would make her whole life completely useless, and she never dreamed that her writing of hymns such as "Take My Life and Let it Be" and "I am Trusting Thee, Lord Jesus" would eventually go down in history and popular appeal as some of the finest British hymns. On an impulse, she wrote what would now be called a "fan letter" to the American writer she admired so much, hoping that somehow it would reach Fanny Crosby's own hand. It did – and that began a distant friendship which became very dear to both women. In one letter, Fanny Havergal wrote:

> *Dear blind sister over the sea,*
> *An English heart goes forth to thee.*
>
> *One in the East and one in the West,*
> *Singing for him whom our souls love best.*

Born in Ireland just two years before Fanny Crosby, the woman who eventually became known by the rather unlikely name of *Cecil Frances Alexander* grew up loving the gospel of Christ and children in equal measure! Throughout her life she had a heart to help children understand the profound truths of the Bible. Although she and her husband moved up the ranks of the church until he was eventually Archbishop of Ireland, Fanny Alexander never lost her wish to inspire children with faith by painting pictures with words. "All Things Bright and Beautiful" was her version of the opening words of the Creed, "I believe in God the Father Almighty, Maker of heaven and earth"; "There is a Green Hill Far Away" was also based on another credal statement, "He suffered under Pontius Pilate, was crucified, dead and buried" – while she wrote "Once in Royal David's City" to explain "Born of the Virgin Mary".

To God Be the Glory

Three women who shared not just a name, but also the gift of words with which they've inspired countless Christians around the world through their hymns. Fired by their deep love of God, they wrote from the heart about their own very human experiences and concerns, touching and lifting the souls of many.

Take myself, and I will be,
Ever, only, all for thee.

AMEN

When I Survey

When I survey the wondrous Cross,
On which the Prince of glory died,
My richest gain I count but loss,
And pour contempt on all my pride.

Were the whole realm of nature mine,
That were a present far too small;
Love so amazing, so divine,
Demands my soul, my life, my all.

(Isaac Watts: 1674–1748)

*L*ove So Amazing – that's the title of this devotional book based on the stories behind our most loved hymns – because in our hymns, above all else, the amazing love of God is expressed in words of wonder, triumph, hope, hardship, fear, sadness, promise, and praise!

Isaac Watts, who created this masterpiece of a hymn, was familiar with all those experiences and emotions. On the face of it, he didn't have a lot going for him. He was just five feet tall with an over-large head and small, piercing eyes. Like all young men, he longed for feminine company, but it seemed the ladies he was drawn to judged him more on looks than character. When he finally plucked up courage to propose to one beloved, she turned him down saying, "I like the jewel but not the setting." That would knock the confidence of anyone, wouldn't it?!

But a real jewel Isaac most certainly was – an intellectually brilliant and deeply emotional man who came to know that the most important intimate and loving relationship in his life was with God. This was in an era when worship in churches was strictly based on doctrine rather than any personal experience of the Christian faith. Isaac, though, had his parents to thank for becoming a free thinker. His scholarly father was twice imprisoned for his nonconformist religious beliefs, so it's not surprising that his questioning son should go on to change the way we worship in church forever.

It began when, like all young boys, young Isaac got bored during the monotone chanting of psalms during worship. His father snapped that if he didn't like it, he should do something about it – so he did! Using his lifelong passion for poetry, he went on to write more than 600 hymns which are regarded as some of the best ever written, earning him recognition as "The Father of English Hymnody". More than that, he broke the mould of hymn writing by including for the first time the personal pronoun "I" to describe the intimate relationship he grew to have with the Lord he loved.

Many people consider "When I Survey" to be the finest of his hymns. Isaac stirs our souls with what feels like such a personal view of Christ's crucifixion that we imagine he was actually standing at the foot of the cross. He lays bare his horror and sadness along with his heartfelt amazement that Christ should go through such suffering for *him* – for *us*! Line by line, he paints a picture of the dreadful reality of Christ's ordeal followed by his questioning of the enormous challenge it presents to *him*. If Christ can give so much for him and for his salvation, then how much more should he be giving in return? He can think of no gift that is great enough. There is nothing to compare. Finally, he proclaims that in small repayment for Christ's sacrifice, *his love so amazing, so divine*, Isaac simply has to offer up everything of worth he has. God's gift of his Son for our sake *demands my soul, my life, my all!*

Isaac Watts knew he had to respond to Christ's unconditional love by dedicating his whole life and soul to God's service.

Faced with the same challenge, what will you give?

Have I the courage? Can I lay aside all the worldly things I think I need, to see clearly the debt I owe to you, O Lord, for the sacrifice your Son, Jesus Christ, made on the cross for me? Such a treasure demands my soul, my life, my all. Open my eyes to what that means, and help me to respond to the amazing gift of your unconditional love with all the devotion, reverence and thanks that should be yours forever.

AMEN

Acknowledgments

Every effort has been made to trace copyright holders and to obtain permission for the use of copyright material. The publisher apologizes for any errors or omissions and would be grateful to be notified of any corrections that should be incorporated in future reprints of this book.

Extract p. 25 taken from the song "Great is Thy Faithfulness" by Thomas O. Chisholm © 1923, Ren. 1951 Hope Publishing Company, Carol Stream, IL 60188. All rights reserved. Used by permission.

Extract p. 40 taken from the song "In Christ Alone" by Stuart Townend/Keith Getty. Copyright © 2001 Thankyou Music/Adm. by CapitolCMGPublishing.com worldwide excl. UK & Europe, adm. by Integritymusic.com, a division of David C. Cook songs@integritymusic.com. Used by permission.

Extracts p. 48 and 50 taken from "Make me a channel of your peace", attributed to St Francis of Assisi, adapted by Sebastian Temple © 1967, OCP Publications.

Extract p. 65 taken from "Forgive our sins, as we forgive" by Rosamond Herklots (1905-87). Verses 1 and 2 reproduced by permission of Oxford University Press. All rights reserved.

Extracts p.110 and 113 taken from "The Servant Song" by Richard Gillard, copyright © Richard Gillard, 1977.

Extract p. 140 taken from the song "Be Still for the Presence of the Lord" by David J. Evans. Copyright ©1986 Thankyou Music/Adm. by CapitolCMGPublishing.com worldwide excl. UK & Europe, adm. by Integritymusic.com, a division of David C. Cook songs@integritymusic.com. Used by permission.

Extract p. 144 taken from the song "How Great Thou Art", words by Stuart K. Hine (1899–1989). Copyright © 1949 and 1953 by the Stuart Hine Trust. All rights in the USA its territories and possessions, except print rights, adm. by Capitol CMG Publishing. USA, North, Central and South America print rights adm. by Hope Publishing Company. All other non US Americas rights adm. by the Stuart Hine Trust. Rest of the world rights adm. by Integrity Music Europe songs@integritymusic.com. Used by permission.